Please return/renew this item by the last date shown.

To renew this item, call **0845 0020777** (automated)
or visit **www.librarieswest.org.uk**

Borrower number and PIN required.

High Tea *in* Mosul

High Tea
in Mosul

The true story of two
Englishwomen in war-torn Iraq

LYNNE O'DONNELL

CYAN

First published in 2007 by Cyan Books, an imprint of

Cyan Communications Limited
119 Wardour Street
London W1F 0UW
United Kingdom
T: +44 (0)20 7565 6120
E: sales@cyanbooks.com

www.cyanbooks.com

All the photographs reproduced in this book were supplied by Pauline and Ali
– to whom many thanks.

A CIP record for this book is available from the British Library

ISBN-13: 978–1-905736–09–6
ISBN-10: 1–905736–09–6

Printed and bound in Great Britain by
TJ International Ltd, Padstow, Cornwall

Contents

Preface

Setting the Scene

It was clear on the morning of April 11, 2003, that Mosul would be the next city to fall under the control of the American military coalition that had invaded Iraq three weeks earlier.

I was staying in Irbil, in Iraqi Kurdistan, along with a few hundred other international reporters who had arrived by various routes, mostly through Turkey and Iran, for a vantage point for covering what was supposed to have been a "northern front." The coalition's initial plan had been to squeeze Saddam Hussein's forces in a pincer from south and north, between the forces that crossed from Kuwait and those that, it had been supposed, would come through Turkey. But the Turkish government, under immense public pressure, declined permission for the use of its bases for US bombing missions and so progress in the north was much slower than expected.

Nevertheless, once they started to fall, the northern cities fell fast. After Kirkuk, the presumptive capital of an independent Kurdistan, Mosul was next.

Travelling in the inestimable care of my driver, Neruddin, a former member of the peshmerga – a Kurdish militia whose name means "those who face death" – I left the Dim Dim Hotel at 6 a.m. and headed towards the smoking plumes rising above Mosul, where looting was already well under way by the time, an hour later, we forced our way through porous Kurdish roadblocks.

As the sun rose over Mosul and the new reality began to dawn, a collective insanity appeared to grip a city that has for millennia prided itself as being at the forefront of civilization. Looting had first been recorded in this part of the world around six hundred years before Christ. The Assyrian empire that had its capital in nearby Nineveh had fallen in the face of a mighty attack that had followed a three-month siege led by the Babylonians and Medes in 612 BC. "The fall of Nineveh, eclipsed in the smoke of an unforgettable conflagration, was the signal for plunder by peoples long suppressed, for violation, greed and revenge," French historian Albert Champdor wrote in *Babylon* in the 1950s. And so it was 2,615 years later in early April 2003. Retribution was nothing new to the Moslawis.

"We need a system here. There is no law and order. The people are upset, they are desperate. But there is no one to bring us security," said a man who approached me when we stopped for a few minutes near the centre of the city. "Now they are taking back what they think has been taken from them." It was to become the day's refrain. A young man pushing a trailer loaded with printers, chairs and desks said he'd taken it all from a state-run cement company. "We are repeating what Saddam did to us. He took money from the people. Now we're taking some of it back," he said.

Everything was up for grabs. If you had a car, you loaded the boot – chairs, tables, refrigerators, sofas and sideboards, paintings. If you had a wheelbarrow, you piled what you could into that – cushions, books, telephones, small tables, stools. If you had a bicycle, you could balance something, perhaps a television, on the saddle and tie a potted plant on the rack. If you had none of the above, you could pull down the curtains and hang them around your neck and use the rod as a walking stick.

A child carried a globe, spinning it on its brass stand as he strode along the middle of a main road. Women, some with headscarves, most without, guarded piles of loot stacked on kerbsides while they waited for their men to return with the means of getting it all home.

It was a free-for-all. For all the disgust that the then US Secretary of Defense, Donald Rumsfeld, generated when asked why the American troops hadn't prevented the looting that saw Baghdad, and other cities across Iraq, stripped bare within days of the allied defeat of Saddam's army – with his dismissive comment: "Stuff happens" – many experts had predicted precisely the scale of the plunder that engulfed the country during the power vacuum that followed the initial stage of the war.

By midday on April 11, the Mosul crowds had torn their way into the main office of the National Bank to take as much cash as they could carry – worthless though the banknotes bearing Saddam's profile were soon to be – but were driven out when one enterprising looter lit a fire so he could keep it all for himself. Outside the bank, I picked an Iraqi military helmet out of the gutter, my only souvenir and one that made me feel uncomfortable for a few hours until we were driving out of the city under sniper fire and I put it on. Neruddin later kept it for himself.

As I headed back to the comfort of the Dim Dim – with hot showers, cold beer, satellite TV and collegial camaraderie – the bridge through the front-line village of Khazer, which had been pounded into dust by the retreating Iraqi army a week or so earlier, was choked with traffic coming towards us as the Kurds of Irbil decided to join in the bonanza under way in Mosul. It was like a picnic day, with carloads of family groups heading towards the biggest party on the block. A carnival atmosphere prevailed. We passed a man driving a tank, standing high in the driver's nest with his head poking up as if from a manhole. He gave the thumbs-up when we waved at him. He told the Italian RAI TV crew that stopped him later in the afternoon that he'd been a tank commander in the Iran–Iraq War but was now a farmer. He had hot-wired the tank to get it started and was taking it home to cannibalize as spare parts for his farm machinery, and use as a plough.

All along the road were the carcasses of donkeys that had been bombed, shot or hit by cars. Others wandered free. Neruddin pointed at them. "Saddam," he said. "Ba'athists." In Arab culture, it is a grave insult indeed to be called a donkey.

This was my introduction to Mosul.

I

High Tea in Mosul

Mosul General Teaching Hospital sits on a hill in the western sector of the city, just beyond the old precinct, and at the end of a wide concrete driveway that sweeps from high steel gates up to smoked-glass doors leading into a foyer. On April 15, when I arrived at around 9 a.m., the gates were still closed after being locked a few days earlier against the looters who had rampaged their way through the city. The hospital authorities had been a little late in introducing such security measures and had lost quite a large quantity of medicines and equipment. There were few people about, but the evidence of still-unexplained gunshot and other wounds was in the blood that lay in pools on the floor of the emergency wards. Nurses in soiled uniforms worked in darkened wards as the electricity was constantly cutting out and fuel for the generators was starting to run low. The place felt dirty, miserable and unsafe.

On an upper floor, senior doctors and heads of department were gathered for their morning meeting. It was here, in the president's large and airy office, that I hoped to be able to get at least part of the picture of what had happened. I had been back in Mosul just a couple of hours, and it was obvious that all authority had dissolved. There were ominous signs that the American military was horribly ill equipped to handle a city in revolt. All Iraqi troops and much of their weaponry had disappeared, and fears began bubbling under that a well-armed Ba'athist-led guerrilla movement was taking shape right here in Mosul.

US Marines had been in and out of the city over the past couple of days, checking on buildings to occupy as their regional headquarters, taking over the airport and bringing in jets and helicopters. Sniper fire on troops in the centre of town on April 11, the first day of Mosul's freedom from Ba'athism, had seen the Americans jump back in their jeeps just minutes after finally turning up, and speed back to their bases in Iraqi Kurdistan. It had been an ominous foretaste of the violent quagmire into which the city, and the rest of the country, was about to descend, as well as a stark example of how the American military reacts to hostility by retreating to its bunker to regroup and come out firing with both barrels. It was clear they had no idea, if they ever had the will, how to win the "hearts and minds" of the Iraqi people whose country they were now occupying.

I had followed along in the wake of a senior Marines officer as he had stomped through the looted building that had been the Mosul governor's office on an inspection tour to assess its suitability as Occupation HQ, crunching along behind him and his entourage through the broken glass and rubble that carpeted the floor. Bored, I went back outside to where his convoy of military jeeps were parked in a neat row outside the building, and where young Marines were standing guard with their legs planted wide and their weapons held high across their chests. A huge crowd, thousands strong and tens deep, was pressing in on a wide perimeter around the quadrangle in front of the governorate building and the inter-sections to the left and right, where sandbags still stood in wedding-cake stacks. The crowd was silent, the people facing the building, watching the Marines and the jeeps, waiting for a sign of authority, for something to celebrate, for some reason to be relieved that Saddam was gone and the Americans had arrived. The atmosphere was tense, expectant, and fraught with a jangling unease.

There was a distant crack, and an American reporter standing 10 metres from me ducked. I looked at the heavily armed twenty-something Marine standing closest to the position I'd taken up behind a jeep and by the small brick wall around the former governor's garden. He was unper-turbed and for a minute I felt reassured by his calm, reasoning that if it had been gunfire, he of all people would have known and would have ducked, too. There was another crack. I dropped down into a squat by the wall and glanced at the Marine, who glanced at me, then at the other Marines, then around at the building, then back at me. We nodded at each other – it was gunfire all right. There were a couple more cracks.

I looked around for my driver Neruddin, as well as the journalists I was working with – Damien McElroy of London's *Sunday Telegraph* and Aart Heering of the Rotterdam-based *Algemeen Dagblad*. Aart, as usual, was talking on the phone to Dutch radio, making one of the many live reports from Iraq that turned him into a household name in Holland. Damien and I started to gingerly make our way towards Neruddin, who had already fired up the engine of our small four-wheel-drive Toyota. "Come on, Aart, we're being shot at," I called. "Aart, come on!" We ran towards the car. "Aart, we're going. Now!" He kept talking into his satellite phone as the Marines emerged from the governorate and ran towards their own jeeps. "AART! NOW!" "I was just saying that I had to go now because my colleagues are telling me that we're coming under fire," he said. Great radio. We dived into our car, I put on the Iraqi helmet I'd picked up in the gutter outside the National Bank, and Neruddin sped us out of there, back to the safety of Irbil, in the Kurdish region, and the Dim Dim Hotel. War was not over after all.

Huge stockpiles of weaponry and ammunition that had been left in empty military barracks and in caches all over the countryside by Iraqi troops – who the Americans had wanted to believe were fleeing for their lives ahead of the all-conquering liberators – were, it was now apparent, in the hands of an enemy unknown and unseen, sinister and frightening, certainly with a specific target and maybe even with a plan. This was the day that a lone sniper on a Mosul rooftop let off a few rounds and let it be known that there was reason to be fearful of what was to come, a potent portent of the utter bloody mess that the country was about to become. That one war may have been "mission accomplished," as American President George W. Bush was to declare from the deck of the aircraft carrier USS *Abraham Lincoln* off the coast of San Diego two weeks later, but another – perhaps even one that had been dormant for decades beneath the jackboot of the dictator – was about to be unleashed.

A few days later, when they had been shot at once more in the centre of town, the Marines opened fire on the crowds of people who still gathered around them on the street. There was little else for people to do: jobs no longer existed as all offices of the government – until the war the country's principal employer – had been closed. Schools and colleges were closed. Shops were closed. According to a French colleague who was in the main square when the Marines started shooting, they had killed and wounded quite a large number of people. The American military later denied the incident had ever happened, but the French journalist had been there, she had seen it. She knew the truth.

In retaliation for the sporadic sniper attacks, the Americans sent enormous Sikorsky helicopters over the city to swoop down on residential areas and major intersections, and hover nose-down, tail-up, with the blades spinning so fearsomely and deafeningly low they were chopping the trees to tabouli. Anyone walking on the streets felt they had to duck to avoid being sliced apart by the apocalyptic war machines or blown off their feet by the force of the gigantic rotors. Tomcat jets roared off the runway of the now-occupied Mosul airport to fly sonic-boom missions across the tops of Mosul's housing estates, low-rise apartment blocks, shuttered souks and schools, over the pulverised remains of the government buildings that had symbolized Saddam's hold on the country – City Hall, the Mukhabarat secret service complex, Saddam's local palaces, police and army HQs, all of which had been destroyed by the smart-bombs of the upgraded American war machine. The jets squealed through the overcast skies at sound- and window-shattering speeds. Canny housewives threw open their windows, practising wartime safety drills to save the glass from splintering in on them.

The whole city, having endured decades of dictatorship, deprivation and dread, the build-up to yet another war and the horror of sustained attack, followed by the confusion of a power vacuum and then days of anarchy and looting, was now being collectively punished for the presence within its midst of some who dared to disdain the invasion and occupation of their country by an army that was so ill prepared for what would and should happen after the fighting was over. A Marine standing guard outside the airport told me – when I asked him where are the engineers, the bridge-builders, the post-war planners, when are they coming? – "Dunno, ma'am. I'm a Marine. I just kill the bad guys."

Outside a school in central Mosul that the Americans had taken over and where they had installed a bunch of pathetic returned exiles who were sitting around smoking, wearing sheepskin jackets and rubber boots, playing at being soldiers of fortune, a Marines officer in a peaked cap had to cup his hands over my ear and shout above the din of the menacing choppers. "Show of force, ma'am," he said. "We do this wherever we go, ma'am. We want them to know who is in control."

So it was on the second floor of Mosul General Teaching Hospital, where the morning meeting of heads of department was breaking up, that I hoped to get some sense of the scale of the problems the Americans were facing, and I was considering approaching the president, who was sitting behind his broad and busy desk at the top of the room, when one of the doctors approached me and, without shaking hands or even introducing himself, asked: "Would you like to meet my wife?"

Yes, of course, I said. As a foreign correspondent, I'd become accustomed to being ignored and overlooked by most of the men I came into contact with in the Middle East and Muslim countries elsewhere, like the "stans" of Central Asia. Some say it is politeness, others that it reflects a culture of misogyny. Sometimes I was regarded as an "honorary man," a device deployed by men who recognized that they were probably going to have to interact with me on terms as close to equal as they could tolerate, and so pretended to themselves that I was, literally, one of the boys. This meant that, by and large, I was able to get my job done. There was a fundamental advantage, too, in being a woman in these situations which did put me ahead of my male colleagues in one important respect, and that was my ability to meet and interact with the women in Muslim countries. And, as I had found, this opened up the hidden half of traditional societies in a way that I couldn't have hoped for otherwise.

And here, in the conference room of Mosul General Teaching Hospital

– four days after the fall of a dictator and as the city appeared to be transforming into an incubator for the anti-American insurgency that was too soon to engulf the country – both sides of that fine dichotomy seemed to be merging. This doctor was about to introduce me to his wife.

He led me outside the conference room, and there, sitting in an alcove behind the door, was a petite and pale, round-faced woman in a long and billowing black dress. "This is my wife," the doctor said.

Hello, I said, offering my hand. How do you do?

Hello, she said. I told her my name, speaking very clearly so she could understand me through what I thought was likely to be an unfamiliar Australian accent. I asked her name. "Pauline," she said.

Oh. I started a little, and may even have laughed. There was something about the way she said it. She was shy, and there was nothing about her mien to suggest she wasn't from around these parts, yet I couldn't be too sure.

Where are you from? I asked her. "Lancashire," she said.

Been here long? "About thirty years," she said. "Would you mind if I used your phone to call my mother? I haven't been able to get in touch with her and she's no idea how we are, whether we're dead or alive. Would you mind? I won't talk for long. I just want to let her know we're all all right."

After an emotional conversation with her mother in Burnley, a world and a war away in the English Pennines, Pauline invited us to her home. There, I met her children, Noor and Jamal, drank copious amounts of tea, patted her dog. We chatted and got to know each other, and I promised, as I headed back out into the traumatized city, to come back for tea later in the week.

My return to Pauline's home three days later was almost an afterthought, as daily movements were set by the news agenda. As such, it was just by chance that I travelled to Mosul that day; I could as easily have headed farther south on Route One towards Tikrit, Saddam Hussein's home town, which had been the scene of great drama in the days following Mosul's fall, as the Americans negotiated with city leaders to crack one of the toughest nuts of the country's capitulation.

Then there was Kirkuk, to the south-east on Route Two out of Irbil. Always a potential trouble spot, Kirkuk is the city that the Kurds claim as their capital. Oil is so abundant in this region – floating as it does on a subterranean sea that represents 7 per cent of total global reserves – that it seeps up through the earth and lies on the surface in huge, greasy, black pools. In this biblical land, it doesn't seem outlandish to believe that the burning bush that gave Moses divine inspiration for his epic journey to the Holy Land was fuelled by the God-given oil that surges in oceanic quantities beneath the Mesopotamian flats. Oil pipelines, long neglected, criss-cross the plains outside the town. On April 18, little more than a week after Kirkuk fell from Ba'athist control, unease was palpable as Kurds began trickling across the former line of control to reclaim homes and farmland that had been seized from them by Saddam and handed over to Arab settlers he had moved in to push the Kurds out.

The details of Saddam Hussein's campaigns against the Kurds are well known – the gassings and disappearances, torture chambers and mass graves, aimed at punishing them for their long-term opposition to his regime, and their intermittent attempts at rising against his brutality. It is difficult to argue against the characterization of his al'Anfal programme as genocidal. But Saddam was now gone, and the Kurds had been living life as they pleased in the protected "no-fly zones" for long enough to have regained a sense of themselves, and to set their sights on revenge and redress. Now Kirkuk was threatening to become a new battleground for Kurdish self-rule aspirations, and the ethnic tensions that were starting to surface between Kurds, Turkomen and Arabs were what many feared could be the first hints of a bloodbath to come. "What the Arabs have sown in the autumn, the Kurds will harvest in the spring," Duilio Giammaria, one of the Italian RAI TV reporters resident at the Dim Dim, said presciently. Kirkuk was simmering.

Nevertheless, the attention of newsroom editors and newspaper readers was turning towards the post-war effort and was now focusing

almost exclusively on Baghdad. But as the looting continued down
south, and American leaders like President Bush and Donald Rumsfeld
continued to talk of freedom and democracy, a nascent insurgency was
beginning to take root in and around Mosul. So that's where I headed
on April 18.

When I arrived at Pauline's home in the mid-afternoon, I couldn't have
been more relieved that I'd decided to drop by, despite Neruddin's reluc-
tance to stay in Mosul any longer than absolutely necessary. He sensed the
danger hanging in the air more keenly than I ever could, and as a Kurd felt
vulnerable to local Arab resentment over the Kurdish vigilantism that had
exploded days earlier, when packs of young men had marauded across the
line of control, often in utility trucks with machine guns mounted on the
cabins, into Arab villages and farms on looting and shooting missions. He
just wanted to go home. But I insisted; we were in the neighbourhood, so
we may as well drop in.

Thank goodness we did. It was immediately clear that for Pauline and
her family, our visit was nothing casual but the highlight of the week,
something they had been preparing for since leaping out of bed that
morning, and for us not to have turned up would have been a devastating
disappointment. We were, as the presence of international correspondents often is for people who have been cut off from the outside world
by dictatorship, repression and war, a sign that things were, possibly
and hopefully, moving back towards some semblance of normality. We
brought news from the outside and we had a fascinated interest in their
lives. As such, we acted as something of a pressure valve for Pauline and
her family – they could relive their experiences, fears and deprivations
with us and we'd never grow bored, or want to change the subject, or try
to outdo them with stories of our own.

For Pauline, too, we were doubly welcome as native English speakers
– we were her people, or as close as was likely to wander in off the street
any time soon. We knew where she'd come from, and where she was
coming from. And we were dripping with satellite phones.

The bustle of anticipation and excitement could be felt through the
locked metal gate as soon as I knocked. The door at the top of the concrete

steps leading up from the street to the house and its large shady garden was pulled open for Pauline to usher us into her home like a mother hen rounding up her chicks, and she proceeded to cluck around us, offering drinks and food and anecdotes, for the next few hours. Her children, 21-year-old Noor and 18-year-old Jamal, kept jumping up from the sofa and running into their bedrooms to bring back gifts – a hand-crocheted doily; a miniature silver Koran cover; a green, heart-shaped stone; a pendant with a desert scene of a camel and an oasis; a pen with gold ink. They thought it was the only way they could show us just how thrilled they were to have us in their home.

Underneath the excited bustle was more than simple hospitality. For these honest and welcoming people, the end of the war, and the end of Saddam, was an event they believed would define their lives ahead. After what they had been through in the past month alone, they seemed content to let their relief burst into joy, and to ignore the omens that were beginning to pile up around them, building slowly in the corners of their lives like dust drifts blown in on a friendless wind.

The table in Pauline's dining room was already laid and the hungry glimpses I stole in its direction from where I was sitting in the drawing room told me that it was groaning with home-cooked food. I imagined that we'd all sit around it, laughing and chatting, breaking bread with our hands, scooping up delicious dollops of home-made hummus and babaganoush with hot-from-the-oven pancakes of fresh white flat bread, piling our plates high with steaming dolma, chickpea salads, tabouli and thick creamy yogurt, sharing the relief of a war's end and the hope of a new normality to come. I could hardly wait.

When it came time to eat, we were directed to our seats around the table, our glasses of fizzy, too-sweet soft drink were replenished, and then the family withdrew to the next room, in traditional Arab style, leaving us gazing at the sad reality of what had, for the past decade or more, been their daily diet. The bread was stale and grey, made with flour of such poor quality that Mosul's bakers had to sift it for stones. The chicken was gristly, tough and tasteless. In place of the succulent salads I'd already tasted in my ravenous imagination, there were platters of colourless, unidentifiable and inedibly hard beans. I looked at Pauline as she was backing out of the dining room but couldn't read what she was thinking. I was honoured to be her guest, and could see that a lot of effort and the warmth of a heartfelt welcome had gone into preparing the table. It was covered in a jaunty cloth, and the food was beautifully presented on glass and ceramic platters. But the food itself looked awful, there was very little of it and I couldn't help wondering whether we were about to eat what would have been the family's main meal of the day. There was no choice. "Please, help yourself," Pauline said. And so we politely, if reluctantly, tucked in with a renewed and humbling awareness of what the people of Iraq had endured – with food scarcities thrown in – for no other reason than because Saddam Hussein was their president.

High tea in Mosul, served up with love and hope, left a bitter after-taste.

"I have to call my girlfriend," Pauline said when we left the table and rejoined her in the drawing room. "If she knows you've been and I didn't tell her so she could come over and meet you, she'll be mad."

Twenty minutes later, a tall, blonde woman smartly dressed in white trousers and a long, pale blue tunic with a lilac chiffon scarf around her neck was standing outside the large plate-glass doors leading to Pauline's garden.

"It's Margaret," Pauline said as she slid the door open to admit her friend.

Margaret is from Durham, an industrial town in the north-east of England. Like Pauline she had married an Iraqi, followed him back to Mosul and lived here for almost thirty years. She had four children, including twin boys, and her eldest, Alia, had married a Jordanian and was living in Amman. Standing later on the stone patio outside the glass doors, she said: "The best thing I ever did was get her out of here." She borrowed a satellite phone to call Alia and let her know that all was well and that, with the end of the war, despite the hysterical eruptions – "It's not as bad as it looks on the telly, love" – they could all start getting on with their lives again.

Unlike Pauline, Margaret had an inscrutable worldliness about her. As she talked, she threw her eyebrows upwards, her chin forwards and her head back, giving the impression that she knew, or at least suspected, more than she was willing to say.

Margaret talked little of the war. That was over; it was time to look ahead. She talked about the neighbourhood mosques, where the faithful had been told that if they'd taken anything that didn't belong to them, everyone would know who they were. Throughout the past few days, the muezzin call to prayer that sounded five times a day from the trumpet-shaped loudspeakers that jostled on the suburban skyline with the star-and-crescent vanes above the ubiquitous onion domes was preceded by the mellifluous voice of the imam telling the anonymous looters that if they didn't want to incur the opprobrium of their neighbours, let alone the wrath of God, they could bring in their loot and nothing more would be said. Both Pauline and Margaret nodded in agreement – this was a good thing. I'd visited some of the mosques and the stuff that was being brought in looked to me as if it was the rubbish that the looters had decided they had no use for – broken coat racks, rickety wardrobes, office chairs with wheels missing from their scratched-chrome legs. Nothing of any use to anyone.

Margaret talked about her elderly mother, Olive, who lived with her in the family home we could see over the wall and down the road from Pauline's garden. Olive was bedridden and not really aware of what the country had just been through. She had Saddam Hussein to thank for being in Iraq at all, Margaret said, as he'd personally intervened with the visa authorities on her behalf. So, not such a bad chap after all? Oh, she wouldn't go that far.

Margaret said her husband Zuhair's car had just been stolen from outside their home. She said it was taken because the number plates identified it as property of the former government – the now discredited, disgraced and dispensed-with Ba'ath Party. While Margaret seemed to believe it was a sign of things to come, Pauline thought that while there might be some initial problems in the new Iraq, such as water shortages and power cuts, it wouldn't be long before life would start getting back to what it had been before all this fuss about Saddam, weapons of mass destruction, sanctions that kept medicines out of hospitals and computer systems in the dark ages of DOS, the oil-for-food programme that seemed to benefit no one but smugglers and bribe-takers, and meant that ordinary people had to chomp their way through gritty rice, ancient chickens and grey bread. It was all up from here, she seemed to think; it was only a matter of time.

Margaret had other ideas. "There's going to be a witch hunt," she said. "Mark my words."

Sitting on the low-backed sofa in Pauline's living room, she turned her head towards her friend, raised her eyebrows, squared her jaw, tilted back her head and added: "But we'll get through it. Inshallah."

2

Romantic Beginnings:
The Road to Iraq

January in Mosul is cold. Snow lies long on the Zagros and Sinjar mountain ranges, which droop down in an arch from Iraq's north-eastern borders with Turkey and Iran. The roads are steep and narrow, and at this time of year can be icy and treacherous as they wind through the mountain passes and skirt deep ravines where the plunge of waterfalls is frozen in time and the knotty vines of some of the oldest vineyards in the home of wine will stand in the field until the spring thaw comes and they are cut back for the next season. The Tigris river originates beyond these mountains, in eastern Turkey, and has fed the rise and fall of civilizations through here for millennia.

The landscape is breathtaking – mountains of untouched ancient forests; deep valleys sliced with rivers painted blue by the peerless sky; lush and sweeping plains that fatten sheep through winter and are burnished throughout the searing summers with the yellow and gold of wheat and oilseed rape. In contrast with the arid plains that stretch to the south-west into the Syrian desert and Jordan, this land is abundant, the unchanging home of Mesopotamia's breadbasket wealth, as the land between the two rivers, the Tigris and the Euphrates that joins it 1,800 kilometres to the south, is the birthplace of modern human life.

It is in these mountains that Pauline's new family have lived for a thousand years, Kurds of the once-nomadic Gerver tribe who trace their roots back to Georgia and whose wanderings took them into Yemen, Iran and southern Turkey. Well before the arrangements made between the Western powers before World War I on the dismemberment of the Ottoman empire, and the eventual divisions that took Mosul out of Turkey, placed it first in Syria and then attached it to Iraq, the Gerver of the Sinjar mountains had adapted to Arab ways.

Newly wed and fresh from a honeymoon in the Syrian town of Aleppo, Pauline was giddy with happiness as she and her husband crossed the border into northern Iraq for the final leg of their journey home to married life in Mosul. In Syria she'd been struck by the beauty of the landscape, and had found the way the rural people lived exotic in its simplicity. Here, though, in what was to be the land of her future, she was shocked by the poverty. And the dreadful thought occurred to her that she might have made a mistake.

"When we first came over the border from Syria after getting married and I saw Ali's village for the first time, I said: 'Please don't tell me we have to live here,'" Pauline said.

As beautiful as it was, she said, the thought of settling down in a thatched mud hut with straw the only insulation against the bitter winter cold and the unbearable summer heat in one of the harshest climates on the planet, and no mod cons, was more than she had bargained for.

"The villages in Iraq were the same as the villages in Syria at that time, all mud huts made out of red clay baked in the sun, thatched roofs sloping over more red clay smoothed across the bricks and dried as hard as concrete, and inside they patched the roof with straw. They were very nice, and cool in the summer, but they didn't have anything – there were no toilets or bathrooms or anything. They were low-rise, just one storey, and long, with lots of rooms. Each group of houses would have a well, and none of the villages at that time had electricity. I said to Ali, please, don't tell me we have to live here."

They were married in Damascus on the last day of January, 1979, after three months of trying, and failing, to get permission for Pauline to travel direct to Iraq. The Iraqi embassy in London kept turning her down – complicated nationalistic and xenophobic domestic politics conspiring to keep many uninvited foreigners out of the country at the time, and as a single woman, what possible reason could she have had for travelling alone to Iraq? So they decided to try neighbouring Syria, where, they thought, they could get married in a simple civil ceremony and then drive over the border as man and wife, fait accompli. "I was given a Syrian visa straight away and I travelled to Damascus on the 29th of January, and Ali and his cousin were there to meet me. The plan was to marry whilst in Syria, but when we went to register, we were told we needed the permission of the Iraqi ambassador. You can imagine our faces. We said to each other that if he didn't agree we would just go back to England and be married there."

To their delight, the ambassador said yes. "And on the 31st of January we were married in the courthouse with Ali's cousin and another relative who lived in Syria as witnesses." An idyllic week driving through Syria, with a few days in Aleppo, went by in a dreamy flash. "I loved Syria in those days, it was so beautiful," she said.

When it was time to head for Mosul, Ali turned the new Volvo he'd bought in England out of the ancient alleys of Aleppo and on to Syria's M4 motorway to the border crossing at Tall-Kucek. The terrain here undulates through villages perched on mounds that rise above the hardscrabble farmland far out of the reach of the fertile grasp of the Tigris. Once over the border and in Iraq, Ali turned on to Route One, Iraq's main north–south highway, and motored across the Nineveh plain until he reached the foot of the Kurdish mountains, where the roads are narrow and potholed: Pauline was terrified as she stole glimpses down the ravines that plunged into the darkness of the deep winter evening. But she was wide eyed, too, with expectation and excitement that made her heart pound and her tiny, white hands clammy with the nervousness she was trying desperately to hide from her husband.

"I saw many villages, but no towns, and they all looked so poor," Pauline said as she recalled the drive through the Sinjar range. Electricity is still to reach much of this region of Iraq; in the late seventies life was lived as it had been for centuries, moving to the rhythm of the seasons, farming families growing only what they needed to get them through to the next harvest. Driving through the land of her husband's ancestors, Pauline was humbled by the simple life the environment forced upon the people who lived here. But mostly, her memories are dominated by the worry that Ali's family would not like her. And, worse, vice versa – or, as she puts it in a dialect undiminished by decades outside her homeland: "What if I don't like?"

It was late on the evening of February 6, the sable sky scattered with stars, when they passed the turn-off for Ali's ancestral village, on the road to the old British oil outpost of Ain Zala and the mountain hamlet of Zammar. As Ali pointed out the place of his birth, visible in the moonlight along the dirt track to the left, and promised a visit soon, Pauline was relieved they were driving on. No lights, no heat, no loo. No thanks. On they went across Nineveh and into Mosul, where the shops lining the streets were strung with coloured lights that reminded her of the Christmas she had just spent at home, and, as they neared their destination, she could see that the whole village had descended from Gerver and were waiting for them at Ali's mother's house. The men started dancing, the women were singing, the crowd surrounded the car clapping and cheering as Ali cruised to a stop and they climbed out into the arms of the Basheer clan. "The women and the children just kept kissing me and putting their arms around me, they loved me from the first step I took into the house," Pauline said. "From that moment, I knew that it would be all right."

Pauline and Margaret came to call this country home in similar ways, meeting and falling in love with Iraqi men who were studying in the industrial north of England in the 1970s. In those days, Iraq was among the wealthiest and most modern of the Middle Eastern states, and though many parts of the country were very poor and backward, the general level of education was high, a large number of people in the towns and cities spoke English, the schools and universities were filled with foreign teachers, and those who belonged to or moved up into the middle classes enjoyed a standard of living comparable at the time to any place in the region.

The two women come from different parts of Britain's industrial heartland – Pauline from Lancashire, Margaret from Durham, areas with proud histories stretching back to the days of the early Britons, and which, each in their way, were among the main engines of wealth and empire that kept the nation chugging along at its peak for more than two centuries. The economies of both regions were already in steep decline by the 1970s, but there were no obvious reasons why women in their twenties, from families that had always been employed and who were both employed themselves, should be anything but optimistic about their own futures. Their families had lived well enough, and lived off the historical fortunes of their respective home towns – directly so in Pauline's case, as both of her parents, her younger sister, and most of her relatives had worked in the Lancashire textile mills that had been the bedrock of the Industrial Revolution, and of Britain's economic and military growth and might, its international clout, its imperial ambitions and acquisitions since the mid-eighteenth century.

Lancashire still brags of the inventors and inventions that it produced at the height of the Industrial Revolution, especially those that accelerated the output of the all-important cotton mills – John Kay's flying shuttle in 1733; James Hargreaves's spinning jenny in 1764; the water frame developed in 1769 by Sir Richard Arkwright, whose family and name came to define one of the most productive eras in England's cotton-milling history; Samuel Crompton's mule in 1779. In the late 1780s, there were an estimated 200 mills in the English counties, Wales and Scotland. By the time the industry peaked just before World War I, in 1912, Britain was producing 8 billion yards of cotton, most of it in the Lancashire mills. Cotton mills dominated the picturesque landscape of England's north-west, and in some areas up to 60 per cent of the population were employed in textiles.

In Colne, one of the many textile villages of the region, Pauline's street was lined with mills. Her descriptions conjure up pictures of rows of identical terraces snaking up and down the streets of a small, clean and neat town settled among rolling green farmland dotted with sheep, juxtaposed with uninhabitable moors shrouded in mist, and where every family in the neighbourhood lives off the local mills; the breadwinners pouring out of their homes together each morning at the blow of the factory whistles; spilling en masse out of the factories to head home again as the whistle-blow signals the end of shift; women with their hair tied in scarves knotted on their foreheads kneeling out of their front doors to scrub the top step; small boys in shorts, caps and woollen coats playing hoop-and-stick up and down the roads. "I used to even wear clogs, the old-fashioned Lancashire clogs with big irons on the bottom," Pauline said.

Pauline's mother was a weaver; her father was what they called a tattler or shedman, responsible for the maintenance of the looms. He spent some time in the dye houses, too, mixing the colours. Her late sister, Mary, never studious, left school at sixteen to work in the mills. Her family was not unusual in that most of her relatives, going back a couple of generations, had worked in the mills. "Some were weavers like my mother, some did other jobs like my father, a tattler and a dyer. All the main cotton mills were on the same road and we lived near by," Pauline said. Had she chosen the same path, she would have been one of the last generation to do so. The real decline of the industry had begun to set in after World War I, when cotton could no longer be exported to overseas markets, and those countries that had been buyers of Lancashire produce began to launch their own domestic industries. Entrepreneurs in India began setting up mills around Bombay producing coarser cotton goods for the domestic Indian market, undercutting the more expensive reimported British product. By the onset of World War II, the Japanese and Americans had set up factories using British technology and expertise, developed in and imported from Lancashire, and in Japan had introduced 24-hour production. Mahatma Gandhi compounded the blow to the Lancashire industry, and by extension the British economy, by calling for a boycott of imported cotton as part of his Indian independence campaign. Mill closures across north-western England accelerated.

A brief reprieve offered by World War II, when mills made uniforms and parachutes – and employment in the industry rose – was short lived even as mill owners absorbed migrants from the subcontinent and began round-the-clock shifts. But their efforts, and legislation in 1959 to reform and consolidate the industry, simply delayed the inevitable. Lancashire's fate had been sealed in 1958, when Britain became a net importer of cotton. The mass production bases of India and China were dominating international demand, and mills across Lancashire were closing so fast that by the time Pauline decided that she wanted to do something else with her life, Lancashire was already a fading dot on the world's textile map – and Colne's mills were simply a part of its once illustrious past.

Pauline had never really been interested in joining the traditional home-town industry anyway; she had an acute sense of place, however, born of her love of history. And Colne has plenty of that. Near by is Pendle Hill, site of a famous witch hunt and hanging in the seventeenth century. And not too far in the other direction, in West Yorkshire, is Haworth, where the Brontë sisters, Emily, Anne and Charlotte, grew up in the parsonage, and where just about every other path, rise, bridge and waterway seems to be called Brontë something, and what's not is said to have featured in a Brontë novel. (Ponden Hall, for instance, an Elizabethan farmhouse, is said to be Thrushcross Grange in Emily's *Wuthering Heights*.) Back in Colne, there is a marble memorial in the main street to Walter Henry Hartley, leader of the quintet aboard the *Titanic* that set up on deck and played popular tunes as the lifeboats were lowered, switching, when it became apparent the end really was nigh, to hymns, which they played to the end.

"I didn't want to go into mills. I was interested in history, Roman and medieval history. I didn't like the Industrial Revolution, which is what we did at school, so I got turned off it and went into nursing instead. There wasn't a lot of unemployment, but you could feel the decline was on the way. In the end, my sister went into a factory that made upholstery for cars. My mother was ready for retirement – she only worked a few years after my father died, which was in March, 1983." Pauline went to nearby Burnley General Hospital to train as a nurse and then joined its intensive care unit, caring for the chronically ill patients there, most of whom were recovering from heart attacks. .

And it was here that she happened upon her future when she met Ali at a hospital dance in 1977 and, soon after, he came to enhance his qualifications, as first a Member and then a Fellow of the Royal College of Physicians, as a heart specialist at the intensive care unit of Burnley General Hospital.

The history of Durham, Margaret's home county, is based on coal. It is a famous cathedral and university city, the medieval buildings of its centre are listed as a world heritage site by UNESCO, and the nearby remains of Hadrian's Wall are evidence of its role as a defensive outpost of the Roman empire. But it is the field of coal that lies beneath the surface which fuelled the growth of the city and the county from the eleventh century, when the prince-bishops who ruled Durham as an autonomous "palatine" encouraged mining for fuel for iron smelting and, around the fourteenth century, heating. While neighbouring Northumberland became the coal-fired engine of the Industrial Revolution, Durham's industry was no less important to the region – at its peak in 1913 the Durham coalfield employed 164,246 men producing 40 million tonnes of coal a year. When the industry was nationalized in 1947, 127 pits employed 108,291 miners producing 24 million tonnes of coal, and though the decline had already set in, post-war reconstruction demand kept the pits open for the next decade. Heavy industries such as iron and steel production, railway engineering and locomotive production (Durham made the first passenger train) and shipbuilding burgeoned on the back of the coal industry. The demise of heavy industry between the world wars hastened after World War II, and led to massive pit closures in the 1960s. The switch to oil as the fuel of the future that had so excited Winston Churchill only accelerated, until by the mid-eighties most of Britain's coal mines were considered uneconomical, the trade unions were regarded, by successive governments, as too powerful, and the resulting political frictions culminated in the coal miners' strike of 1984/85. Durham's last pit closed in 1985.

Many communities were shattered by the strike and the death of coal mining, as well as the allied businesses that sprang up on the back of the industry, such as transport and haulage, equipment suppliers, village shops. Government financial support helped develop light industries like electronics, and the city's reputation as a seat of learning remained untarnished; Durham University is considered one of the best in Britain.

Despite her father being a coal miner, Margaret has never felt the fate of the industry as part of her own destiny. By the time she was growing up in Consett, a mining and smelting centre in Durham, the place had long since become what she describes as a "ghost town," with the closure of the iron and steel works years earlier and the incremental closure of the collieries. Her parents separated when she was eight and there was no contact with her father or any of his relatives after that. When she was eighteen, she and her mother and younger brother moved to Newcastle to comply with a court-ordered condition of an uncle's divorce: a judge had decided that the uncle could have custody of his three children only if his sister, Margaret's mother Olive, lived close enough to help take care of them. So they moved to nearby Newcastle and Olive became surrogate mother to another three children.

"Mam had a very tough life," Margaret said of Olive, who at fourteen went into service in a "posh house" as a kitchen maid, and at seventeen went to work in a Consett steelworks where she met her future husband. At twenty she was married, and by 28 she was the single mother of three children. "She brought us up on her own, and then there were the other kids to look after once we were off her hands, so it never really seemed to end for her," Margaret said.

A couple of years before they moved to Newcastle, Margaret left school, aged sixteen, to help her mother make ends meet. "I went to a secondary modern school and did the GCEs, so I got my O levels. And then I took the civil service exam and I passed that. Soon after, I got my GCE results and I had five O levels, which meant that I could be a clerical officer. I went to work in Newcastle and they trained me."

It was on a night out with girlfriends from the Pensions Department that Margaret met Zuhair, and life changed for ever.

Margaret and Zuhair are sitting on the white faux-leather sofa in the sitting room of their first-floor flat in Penge, a dormitory suburb in southeast London, where the street names echo a past association with royalty, and not far from where Sir Joseph Paxton's Crystal Palace was rebuilt following its huge success in Hyde Park for the Great Exhibition in 1851 showcasing the finest that the British Empire, then at its peak, had to offer.

The flat is on the two upper storeys of a three-storey house in the middle of a long row. It's a short walk from the train station and a shopping centre. It has been recently renovated; Margaret is its first occupant since the bathroom and kitchen were refitted and the place was recarpeted, though she is at a loss to understand why anyone in their right mind would lay thick white carpet in a rental flat. She's got most of it covered with protective mats, terrified that she'll have to pay enormous amounts to have it cleaned, or, worse, replaced when it comes time to leave. She doesn't need to have been in London long to know that (a) the tenant always loses; and (b) everything in London ends up costing more than you could have imagined.

Zuhair has come for a short visit from Yemen, where he is a lecturer at a university in the picturesque and pious town of Ibb, in the country's south-western highlands. He doesn't seem to like the job very much, and he finds it tedious that his female students are so severely sequestered behind the veil of their religion that they even wear gloves and, in some cases, sunglasses in class. He has put signs on their desks, he says, so he knows whom he is addressing. He finds the weather nice, the air clean, his colleagues respectful. But without his family, he is lonely. It is clear he misses Margaret terribly.

"My hubby," Margaret says as she introduces him. They haven't seen each other for a few months and are thrilled to be together, however briefly. Zuhair reclines on the sofa in his stockinged feet, smoking and watching his wife. He looks severe, watchful, almost distrusting – until he smiles. Then his face lights up and his eyes crinkle with warmth. Margaret sits down beside him. And their story begins.

Zuhair: We met in 1971, in Newcastle University, or a place near there. I was studying zoology on a scholarship from Mosul University. I arrived on December 18, 1970. I started my course work in January.

Margaret: We met at the student union at the university. I was with girl-friends, drinking, on a girls' night out. We were standing around in a group, just talking. And he was there with a group of friends, too, just talking. And then Zuhair and I just started talking. It was the 9th of April. Someone was having a party over Easter time two or three days later, on the Monday. After that, a week or so later, he invited me for dolma.

Zuhair: No, it was an Indian restaurant.

Margaret: We always used to go to Indian restaurants. We saw each other once a week, as Zuhair spent a lot of time by the seaside, at a marine biology lab.

So, did romance blossom?

Margaret: [laughs] I never thought about the cultural differences. *She turns to Zuhair.* When you left to come to the university, your mam said: "Don't you go marrying a foreigner." But that was because one of the relatives married a Turkish lady and she wasn't very clean and she [Zuhair's mother] thought we were all like that. But as soon as she knew that Zuhair was happy, she was all right.

Zuhair: I went home in 1975 to Mosul, and came back to England in December 1976.

Margaret: We had a mosque marriage, which was recognized religiously but not civilly. We weren't married civilly in England or Iraq until December 1977. We still lived apart, because we had to be careful. The religious ceremony was in a Pakistani mosque which I think at that time was a converted house. It was in 1973. We never lived together while he was a student in England but saw each other regularly like any normal couple at that time. I lived with my family and Zuhair lived in a student house. We used to have some really good parties there. I would often go there for meals as Zuhair is a good cook, and we'd invite our friends as well. Alternatively he would come and spend time at my family's home.

Zuhair: It was a condition of the scholarship that we could not get married to foreigners, and they passed a law saying you couldn't get a job if you did.

Margaret: He got his degree in 1975, went home and worked for a year. Then he came back over to England and we got married in July. I can never remember if it was the 26th or 27th.

Zuhair: Twenty-seventh.

Margaret: Then Zuhair went home again and came back in July 1977, when I had a holiday. When he came over in 1975, he bought a Mercedes, and picked it up in Rotterdam, so when he was leaving, we left from Hull by ferry, went to Rotterdam to pick up the car, and we drove through Europe to Turkey, camping. His cousin travelled with us. It was lovely. We had a nice holiday. We did it for a month – Rotterdam, Amsterdam, Cologne, Munich, Frankfurt and Salzburg. Zuhair then went on to Dubrovnik and Split. We stayed a week by the Adriatic. Then to Bulgaria overnight and to Istanbul for a week.

You could hardly call it a honeymoon as we had Zuhair's cousin with us as well. A few months prior to Zuhair finishing his PhD one of his cousins had his foot blown off when he stepped on a mine in Kurdistan – he was in the army. So he was sent to England for treatment, and his brother also travelled with him. The one who came for treatment had to have his leg amputated from above the knee and was waiting for an artificial leg. He was going to fly home to Iraq and his brother came with us. It was a fantastic experience for me – I went as far as Turkey with Zuhair then I flew home while Zuhair and his cousin continued their journey through Syria to Iraq.

I always think of my honeymoon as being after my civil wedding when we went touring around Scotland. We booked a place in Stirlingshire, I think, which had a waterbed. My friends and family had put a fish on the engine and pennies in the hubcaps so I don't know how many times we stopped because of the noise and the smell. That for me was my special day as we had my family and friends, and Zuhair's tutor and family sharing it with us. We had a nice reception in a hotel in Jesmond, then my mam did a party in the evening in our house.

After her first trip through Europe with Zuhair and his cousin, Margaret returned to Newcastle from Istanbul while Zuhair drove through Syria on the M4, crossing into Iraq at Tall-Kuchek, through the Sinjar mountains on Route One to Mosul. He got back well before the government cancelled the tax concessions on imported new cars, and he received a block of land as a returned scholar.

Two years later, he drove back to Newcastle to collect Margaret and bring her home as his bride. He bought a caravan for a cousin, hooked it up to the Mercedes and they filled it with what they thought they would need for their new life – including the kitchen cabinets that would be fitted in the home they planned to build together. It was important to Margaret, she said, that she have a good kitchen.

The trip back was once again like a camping holiday, only this time they didn't stop in Istanbul but took to the highways that stretch across eastern Turkey, through the rugged, poverty-stricken Kurdish region. The landscape is dizzying – much of it is flat and expansive, covered in rubble that, to one gazing out of the window of a speeding car, appears to move in eddying swirls. Now and then, this mesmerizing kaleidoscope is broken up by an acre or two of land that has been cleared and the boundaries marked out by larger rocks; it is said that if you can endure the back-breaking work of clearing a plot of rocks to reveal the fertile soil below, then it's yours. The names of the towns hint at the history of settlement, many ending in "tepe," which refers to the mounds created as one village crumbles with age and another is built on its ruins. In those days, when Margaret and Zuhair were towing their caravan east towards Mosul, the borders were easily crossed and the Kurdish families scattered over Iraq, Turkey and Syria, the three countries that merge here, had easy contact. These days, the border is delineated by barbed wire, closed crossings and, in Turkey's case, a military presence reinforced from nearby army and air force bases. What hasn't changed is the comparable quality of the roads; the Turks know the importance of good roads to their military efficiency and invest the money and manpower in maintaining them. Between Istanbul and the Harbur Gate crossing into autonomous Iraqi Kurdistan, tiny Silopi is the last town on the Turkish side; over the border, the road slides through the Zagros mountains, and the next stop is Dohuk, proud home of the best supermarket in the country.

Margaret: In 1977 we went all the way through Turkey ...

Zuhair: I didn't want to go back via Syria because the roads weren't good.

Margaret: We didn't have an air conditioner in the car, so it was so hot we used to put wet towels on our heads. We went straight through, we didn't go to the seaside. We were towing the caravan, which was great. We slept in it, and it was full of stuff – kitchen cabinets, books, wedding presents. Things we were taking back with us.

I wasn't nervous. It was bad leaving my mam behind. She came as far as Dorset with us. We left her with our brother. That was the worst thing, leaving behind my mam and family.

All of Zuhair's family were in Dohuk waiting for us. We went through at Harbur. All the family were there, they had their cars and they were tooting their horns, and clapping and singing – all the men and the children came up to greet us and welcome us home. Most of the women had stayed behind so I met them when we got back to Mosul.

Luma, Zuhair's youngest sister, was there at Dohuk. She was still little then, just ten years old. I remember she took my hand, and that was it. That was it.

All the ladies were waiting in the family house. Everything was white, with white embroidered covers on the furniture, and the courtyard, and the food, and everybody was there, all the women.

I had rubber sandals on my feet because I'd fallen over in Turkey and hurt my foot so I couldn't wear proper shoes. I felt a bit embarrassed about that, and still do when I think of it, and how I must have looked. I wasn't dressed up as a bride, even though I was coming home as a bride. I was thin because I'd been sick in Turkey, too. And I couldn't help feeling that I must have looked like a beetroot.

3

A Boiled Sheep's Head Too Far

The Japanese have sea urchin, the French have andouillette. The Chinese have chicken's feet and the Scottish have haggis. For Iraqis, it's patcha. For Margaret and Pauline, patcha was a boiled sheep's head too far.

Recipe for Patcha

Ingredients
1 sheep's head
½ kg of minced meat
½ kg of lamb chops
2 sheep's stomachs
Intestines of one sheep
1 cup of chickpeas (soaked overnight)
2 cups of rice
Mixed spices – coriander and cumin
Salt and black pepper

The day before you plan to serve the patcha, clean the intestines by running cold water through them to flush out any residual "debris," as Pauline calls it. Then leave them to soak overnight.

Method

Ask the butcher to clean the sheep's head.

Add the mincemeat to the rice. Season with salt and mixed spices.

Wash the stomachs and the intestines.

Cut the intestines into three and fill each piece with the rice-meat mixture.

Tie each end of the filled intestines with cotton thread, and put to one side.

Fill the stomachs with the rice-meat mixture. Use the cotton thread to sew them closed. Put them to one side.

Place the sheep's head, stomachs, intestines and lamb chops into a very large pot.

Add the chickpeas, salt and pepper, and cover with water.

Cook on a medium heat for about two hours, until the meat is tender.

Serve on flat bread with lemon wedges.

You will need a clean hammer, and a strong stomach of your own, to crack open the skull. Scoop out the brains. Eat. Enjoy.

"I refuse to eat this," said Pauline, point blank. So did Margaret.

Like the Japanese, French, Chinese and Scottish when it comes to the extreme exoticism of their culinary peccadilloes, no one in Mosul seemed to mind that the new arrivals couldn't stomach the sheep's brains and guts. Pauline has to leave the room when it comes to the hammering of the head to reach the mushy broiled brains – though she says Ali and Noor "go crazy for it." Margaret's late mother-in-law always made something else for her when patcha was on.

Sheep are central to Iraqi cooking – preferably old and fat – and very little gets thrown away. There's not much to tell Iraqi food apart from that of the rest of the Middle East – like the people and their culture, the food is a pastiche of traditions and history stretching back thousands of years through migration, invasion, siege and settlement; boundaries drawn, erased and redrawn; occupation and disintegration; drought, flood, famine and plenty; natural calamity and political calumny. Everyone who came through brought a little extra with them.

Agriculture can be traced back 8,000 years or more between the two rivers. Wheat, barley and rice are the staples, along with corn and millet, sugar and oilseeds. Until recently vegetables and fruit were seasonal – no such luxuries as tinned pears or frozen peas. Everything was bought when it was available, and if you thought you'd need tomatoes during the winter, you pulped them yourself, and after drying the pulp in trays laid out in the sun on the roof, froze enough to get you through to next season.

Pauline was surprised by this comparative scarcity and the hard work that came with it, and she had to get used to cooking with the produce available when she shopped – root vegetables in winter, leafy vegetables and stone fruit in summer.

Patcha aside, there's plenty to like about the food, and that was especially true during the seventies and eighties, before international sanctions led to widespread shortages. The transition for Pauline and Margaret from the land of meat and two veg, in northern England, to the land of mutton and rice, in northern Iraq, was never going to pivot on how well they took to the food. It was, however, because of food – or, rather, the lack of one particular food – that they became aware of their Englishness. They had arrived believing themselves to be modern, seventies women, breaking out of the provincial mould and heading for exotic, faraway climes, members of the new polyglot generation that had consolidated the Western social upheaval of the previous decade, citizens of the world unbound by anyone's definition of them as "English" ... Until, that is, they couldn't find potatoes.

"It was such a shock to me that we couldn't get potatoes," said Pauline, "because I was brought up on them. I mean, I love rice. But I *love* potatoes. And when you have an English dinner, you want to have potatoes, don't you?"

And so was born the Annual Potato Frenzy, a fortnight of every year, in mid-May, when Pauline and Margaret, and the handful of other Western women in Mosul who had married Iraqi men and who made up a solid pack of close friends, would drop everything in their quest for a potato. "They were only available for two weeks a year and if we saw them out we'd call each other up and say I saw potatoes at such and such a place," Pauline said, laughing.

Potatoes are not completely unknown in Iraq, and most that were grown in the country when Pauline and Margaret first arrived were produced on small farms close to Mosul. The climate, with summer temperatures above 45 degrees Celsius, and the lack of proper storage facilities meant that a lot of the crop rotted before it got to market. But the farmers didn't care because they mostly grew potatoes just to fill in time between beans.

"They weren't very good quality, many were bad and they weren't very nice, but we made do," said Pauline of the Mosul spuds.

Margaret agreed. "We used to laugh and say who would think we'd be going crazy over a sack of potatoes. But there we were, going crazy for potatoes."

It was the same with most things in those days – white sports socks, Cadbury's chocolate Flakes, packets of instant noodles with flavour sachets, news that a women's clothing store had opened up on Nineveh Street and had smart black trousers in stock. If they were out and saw something that wasn't normally available, they bought it, either for themselves or for their girlfriends. "Because you'd never see it again," Pauline said.

Mosul potatoes might not have been the waxy orbs they preferred, but mashed with lots of butter and plenty of salt, they were a good enough accompaniment for the home-style dinners the Englishwomen of Mosul couldn't live without.

⁂

Unconditional love and support were the greatest assets that Margaret and Pauline had in the early days of their new lives. The patience and understanding of their husbands and families provided them with a solid platform from which to negotiate what were often strange – and strict – customs and expectations. Change comes slowly to this part of the world, and central to the transition for the two Englishwomen was learning just how different they were – and how different they could remain.

Margaret married into a family of comfortably off Arab intellectuals; many of Pauline's new relatives were farming people who lived by mores unchanged for centuries. Nevertheless, the pressures that each of the Englishwomen faced as they grappled with the duties, responsibilities and obligations of their roles as Iraqi wives were similar in many ways because of the efforts of their husbands to ensure that the changes in their lives did not lead to a change in the women they had fallen in love with and brought home. In Pauline's case, pressure from her husband's family to conform to their way of dress and their habit of sequestering women indoors was firmly resisted by Ali. Zuhair, secular and liberal, believes Margaret was overcautious and excessively modest in the early years. The unwavering respect that each man has for his wife as an individual, as well as for the culture and country that she had left behind, was fundamental and paramount to the enduring success of their marriages.

They were not by any means unique – many Iraqi men who had studied abroad returned with foreign wives. But Pauline and Margaret watched many of these marriages disintegrate under a variety of unforeseen strains and counted off their girlfriends as many women gave up and went home or moved elsewhere in the region, where they found the cultural and political pressures easier to negotiate than the evolving conservatism in Saddam's Iraq. Many others left in the early years of the war with Iran, and even the small number who returned when that senseless episode finally ended in 1988 left once more when Saddam invaded Kuwait in 1990 and the drums of war again began pounding.

"I was lucky. I still feel very lucky, because a lot of my friends' husbands changed when they came back," said Pauline. Many returning Iraqi men "clung to their religion," she said, forcing their Western wives behind the veil, or at the very least to wear headscarves in what was a largely secular society that neither demanded nor expected it. Some women did not like the obligations of a large, extended and intrusive family. Or the way in which Arab families interact with each other, constantly in and out of each other's homes and lives in a gregarious spirit of "what is yours is mine and everybody else's, too."

Pondering her own fortune, Margaret adds: "There were other foreign girls who didn't have such a good time – some marriages didn't last, either because the mothers-in-law were possessive of their sons and not so welcoming, or the wives preferred to be isolated, spending time just as a couple or a small family rather than in the collective kind of way that Arab families live in. I didn't. I preferred to be with the family. A lot of the men brought wives back and a lot didn't work out. So, seeing other women have a difficult time, it made me realize how lucky I was. I never had any problems."

Pauline had never doubted that leaving her home and family to travel across the world with Ali, to a country she had never visited and a life she could not even begin to imagine, was the right thing to do. And no one close to her back in Lancashire ever had any doubts, mainly, she said, because of the high regard they had for Ali. "Apart from being sad that we were leaving England and would be a long way away, there was no one saying don't go, because they loved him. My father and mother just loved him. There were no objections because they loved him, all the family; they just got along fabulously with him. I never had any problems, any snide remarks about going out with a foreigner. Anywhere he was, people just liked him because he's kind, always considerate and helping people.

"Ali is such a nice person to everyone, that everyone who met him liked him instantly. He is always generous and unselfish. I'll give you an example – at the hospital, he never took the extra money at the end of the month for doing the death certificates. This money was supposed to be added on to his salary, an extra fee for attending deaths and signing the certificates, but he always took the money and bought cake and other presents for the secretaries of the consultants and other staff. He's just like that. And there were no objections to me coming here because they all knew that he would look after me."

With the initial joy of their homecoming, and the wonderful shock for Pauline of being immediately welcomed into this huge family, she was treated like a princess for the following four months while she and Ali lived with one of his many cousins. "They wouldn't let me do anything, housework or cooking or anything. They were just great to me. I'd rather have got involved because it was boring otherwise. But I read a lot, and learned a lot."

Learning the history of Mosul, of Iraq and of the Middle East through reading and visiting local landmarks and museums was one thing. Becoming part of a familial fabric was another. Pauline found it difficult being accompanied by male relatives wherever she went. The women of Ali's clan rarely left their homes other than for family outings, and the idea of the women working outside the home would just never have entered anyone's mind. "But the house was very big and had two very big gardens which were beautiful; I enjoyed spending time in them."

The Eastern-style toilet – over which one squats – was a challenge: "I didn't like it at all, it was very difficult at first, but after a while, as with everything else, you adjust."

Watching television was not an option – programming was almost exclusively geared towards promoting the government of Saddam Hussein. The few television and radio stations were controlled by the Ba'ath Party, which, like dictatorships from China and North Korea to Zimbabwe and Belarus, used them to shape the opinions of a population starved of other sources of information. Often, the same programme would be broadcast on rotation for days on end. There were few serials, fewer movies that weren't lionizing Saddam, and the purpose of news programmes was to proclaim Iraq as the land of milk and honey whose people had the great fortune of being watched over by a benign and loving father. The tone of media coverage changed according to the political situation – during the war with Iran, for instance, and after international sanctions were imposed on Iraq, when external forces were demonized and Saddam was portrayed as a godlike figure heroically holding back the tide of enemies at the gates.

This sort of bombardment of dross numbs the critical faculties and hardly provides compelling viewing. So, people went out, visiting, picnicking on the banks of the Tigris until one or two o'clock in the morning in spring and summer, holding barbecues at home, prom-enading along Nineveh Street, piling into their cars and, when the lowland temperatures became insufferable, heading to the cooler Sinjar hills and the Swiss-style chalets built there by the government tourist authorities.

But Pauline soon discovered that this, too, could wear on the nerves, as Ali's relatives would drop by at all hours of the day and night and treat her home as their own. As many of the relatives were farmers, between planting and harvest they had little to do. "They'd sleep in the afternoons, and relax. And then basically they're bored, so they come visiting. And think nothing of ringing your doorbell at nine o'clock at night," Pauline said. "You're just getting ready to go to bed, and the doorbell goes and it's a relative dropping by for a cup of coffee. And they'd stay until eleven, twelve o'clock at night. I couldn't believe it and it used to make my blood boil. I remember, soon after I first got here, we were having some people over to dinner, and out of the blue this young married couple turned up – cousins, of course – at dinnertime. There wasn't enough food for them as well, because I'd prepared for a dinner party, so these two just went into the kitchen and started cooking for themselves. I couldn't believe it. I said to Ali, what do they think they're doing? We're having people for dinner and they're in the kitchen cooking for themselves. And he just laughed and said, oh, you'll get used to it.

"The relatives here, they just think that your house is their house and they can come and go as they please. Now they're a bit older they don't go out so much. And there's the curfew, of course." The quid pro quo is that "if I need them, they're there. So it's not that bad, but they do have this habit of just turning up," Pauline said, laughing.

If it's a two-way street within the family, though, the same cannot be said of neighbours who prevailed on Ali's generous nature to drop over for free consultations, or stop him on the street for medical advice. Working long hours to establish his clinic, holding down his position in the university's cardiology department, and as breadwinner for a young and growing family, Ali found the 24 hours in his day all spoken for. But no sooner was he home in the evening than the doorbell would ring and a neighbour would be standing outside with a request that he come straight over because a child had taken ill, or a grandparent was feeling poorly. On Fridays, his only day off, he couldn't walk down his street without being stopped for an impromptu consultation. And when he stayed at home, his erstwhile patients would simply ring his bell and demand his time – all for free, of course – rather than go to the clinic. Pauline's annoyance levels rose and her tolerance levels fell with every ring of the bell. But Ali found it impossible to refuse.

Money didn't come easily in the early days of Pauline and Ali's married life. With government policies constantly changing, he had been too late to take advantage of some of the tax concessions and benefits offered returning students. He had to pay import duty on the Volvo, for instance, as the regulations changed before he got it home. He'd missed out, too, on free land that had been handed out to many upon their return.

His Mosul University salary was not enough to rent a house in a market where landlords demand up to a year's rent, in cash, in advance. But staying with relatives for the first year or so after he returned to Mosul with Pauline allowed Ali to save enough to open his own clinic. Soon after Pauline joined him, the clinic was doing well and Ali was beginning to feel well on the way towards financial stability. In mid-1979, they found a cosy house, put down a year's rent, and moved in. With the help of both their families they furnished it. Pauline's father sent them the money to buy a washing machine, which until just a year earlier had not been available in Mosul as washing was generally done by laundrymen, who collected and delivered. Soon after moving in, they learned that their first child was on the way.

"They were happy days in the beginning," Pauline said. "I always remember those days as happy days. We had a little money box and at the end of the month we'd open it up and get the money out and go for pancakes. And there was a newsagent's where I could get *Woman* and *Woman's Own*, so we'd bring the pancakes back and I'd have a *Woman* and a *Woman's Own* and we were content. There was some struggle. But life is like that sometimes, you have a bit of a struggle."

Not everyone in Mosul was struggling at the time, Pauline is quick to point out. But Ali's father had died when he was a toddler, his mother never remarried and their welfare became the responsibility of his father's brothers. From the fifties, the Iraqi government began sending top students to Western universities, particularly in Britain and the United States, to complete undergraduate or postgraduate studies, covering their living costs and offering them financial and tax incentives to return. After the Ba'ath Party took control of the country in the late sixties, the policy continued, but as strong nationalistic winds were blowing through Iraq, stringent conditions were attached to the scholarships, with marriage to foreigners forbidden. While the authorities were generally seen as turning a blind eye on scholarship students who did return with foreign wives – though Zuhair took the precaution of waiting a year or two before bringing Margaret home, just to be sure – some were turned in and lost their jobs. In contrast to Zuhair's situation, though, Ali's uncles paid for most of his education, sending him, after he had completed medical school in Mosul, to London, Burnley and Northern Ireland. One uncle even travelled to Burnley, alone, his first time ever outside Iraq, to deliver a hamper of food, so concerned was the family in Gerver that Ali might be homesick and not eating properly.

Once their new home was furnished, Pauline returned to Lancashire, in September 1979, to prepare for Noor's birth. The standards of hospital care were not as high in Iraq as in England and Pauline was not yet comfortably proficient in Arabic. She wanted to be near her parents, and she wanted her children to have British citizenship. "If they decided when they were older that they wanted to live and study in England, that would make it easier for them," she says. She returned in February, 1980, with a three-month-old baby. Soon after, Mosul University allocated Ali a small flat on a hilltop overlooking the city. "It was beautiful, you could see all of Mosul," she says.

Becoming a member of Ali's family was like entering a honeycomb of such linguistic and cultural diversity that Pauline's head didn't stop spinning for months. She found herself among a huge, extended clan whose many members welcomed her warmly, and fussed over her for months, but who had been taken by surprise at her very existence, as the tradition of marrying within the family had been unbroken for more generations than could be counted back. Ali had bucked the practice by taking a bride from outside the fold. But there was good reason for him to do so as the devastating consequences of marrying within the family, generation after generation, were apparent for all to see. The natural manifestation of genetic degradation resulting from cousin marrying cousin was the sole reason why Ali had never intended, once he understood the science of genetics, to marry in.

One cousin who had believed herself to be the designated bride for Ali "was a bit awful at first," Pauline says, "nothing nasty, she just rarely communicated with me. She's a lot better now than she used to be. But she's still not married."

It's not at all certain that first cousins will produce children with genetic disorders and diseases, but British experts do generally put the risk 50 per cent higher, at 3 per cent, than the 2 per cent for the general population, in which cousin marriages are unusual. The risk increases, though, when cousin marriages go back many generations, as they do as a tradition in close-knit, tribal societies like those in Pakistan, Saudi Arabia and Iraq. As most people in the clan are related, all four parents of a cousin marriage are likely to be close relations, as were their parents. With each generation, the risk increases that what should be throwback genes will come to the fore and, with time, become dominant.

This appears to be the case in Ali's family, as genetic disorders that were once carried only by the females are now also being carried by the male side, and in some cases are indeed showing as dominant.

Pauline described the problems in Ali's family, citing blood and muscular diseases, learning difficulties, mental retardation and degenerative mental and physical disorders, and said that with genes once carried only by the women now also showing up in the men, some large families in the clan had four or five children out of a total of ten or twelve with muscular dystrophy, motor neurone problems and learning difficulties of varying severity. The two children born to one couple, both boys, had motor neurone disease. Two of Ali's aunts, his mother's sisters, died of genetic diseases. Both the male and female sides of the family had, for at least the past three generations, passed on defective and formerly recessive genes.

Ali had seen it coming. In a couple of cases, he had begged his cousins not to have more children. One cousin was a doctor, "and Ali was very angry with him, telling him he should have known better. But it made no difference. They like to marry within the family," Pauline said.

So much do they like to keep everything within the family that Ali warned Pauline, as soon as Noor was born, not to even joke about betrothing her. "Ali told me when Noor was still a baby – if anyone says Noor is for our son, even as a joke, don't say yes. Because if you say yes, that's it. They are very tribal; they never forget, and we'd be in for trouble."

Ali's family like trouble, she said, and it came their way despite their best efforts to deflect it. Once Noor reached marrying age, some cousins started fighting over her, without even consulting Pauline and Ali. Noor had other ideas, having fallen for the man who would become her husband, and her future mother-in-law had to be sworn, reluctantly, to secrecy until everything was formalized, in order to avoid retribution.

Pauline had seen what the relatives could be like and knew that secrecy was essential for her family's safety.

"There was a great-uncle – the head of the clan in Iraq – who was very rich and owned a lot of stalls in the souk. His son wanted a particular cousin and had set his sights on her and just assumed that she would be his. But, like Noor, she had other ideas and she went with another boy. Well, when she was given out, the great-uncle and his son and a crowd of others in the family came around with guns and shot up the house! While they were all in it! And they're all relatives! Oh, Ali's family like trouble all right."

One hapless woman was forced to marry a cousin she not only didn't want to spend her life with but whom she loathed the sight of. But she had been betrothed to him as a baby and for his family a promise was to be kept. "She was prevented from marrying anyone else because she'd been promised to him. And she hates him, just hates him. But in the end she had to marry him because there was no one else. She's forty-five now, and very unhappy."

Word of Noor's impending engagement had to be kept quiet until it was formalized in a traditional ceremony to make sure that no one in Ali's family could prevent it. "The relatives didn't speak to us for a year, and some still don't. But, as Ali said, no loss," Pauline said.

The tribalism of the clan spilled into pressure on Pauline to adopt their dress and their mores, including living separately from the men. She was expected to cover her head, eat only with the women, stay indoors at all times, and certainly not to work outside the home. "Ali said no. He wouldn't have it. He used to say, 'No, it's not what she's used to, she stays with me.' They respected Ali; whatever he said, they'd do. He was the most educated, he'd been abroad, and they were so interested in England and wanted to know so much."

4

From Jonah to Saddam

City of Sin

The story of Jonah begins and ends in Mosul – or the outer reaches of Nineveh, as it was in his day, in the eighth century before Christ.

Jonah was a resentful prophet who almost died trying to defy God's command that he tell the people of Nineveh that unless they changed their sinful ways their city and everything in it would be destroyed. Much of Jonah's story is set down in the eponymous Old Testament book – with mentions in the Koran – that provides an allegorical precursor to the experiences of Jesus more than eight hundred years later, and bears witness to a benevolent and patient God.

In those days, Nineveh was one of the richest and most important cities in civilization, with a population of 120,000 people and, according to the Bible's not always cosmopolitan perspective, a lot of cattle. Massive crenellated walls that in some places were 45 metres thick protected it. Fifteen gates – some of them arched, some built partly of stone, and one in particular, the Nergal Gate, flanked by massive bulls that were the chosen symbol of power for the Assyrian kings – served as entrances to the city. The Shamash Gate could be approached only by crossing bridges over moats. Water was abundant, channelled by canals and viaducts from the nearby mountains, and agriculture – grain, fruit, vines – had been long established and irrigated from the Tigris, on whose eastern bank the city sat. By Jonah's day, Nineveh was a centre of intricate workmanship, notably ceramics, metalwork and sculpture. The Assyrians had sophisticated visions of civic design and laid out the city with sweeping boulevards and piazzas, and public parks and gardens that showcased trees and flowers from as far as the empire stretched. King Sennacherib, who moved the Assyrian capital to Nineveh from nearby Nimrud around 700 BC and who died in 681 BC, built himself a magnificent palace that, according to descriptions of the day, made use of a vast range of materials from across the great swath of territory under his sway. As the hub of a busy trading culture, Nineveh buzzed with camel trains and barges carrying the booty of the far-flung fiefdoms – gold, silver, copper, red sandstone, alabaster, ivory, a huge variety of timbers, enamelled bricks, limestone. Sennacherib funnelled the treasures of his empire into his fabulous palace, which was spread over thousands of square feet, with at least 27 entrances – guarded by winged bulls, carved in alabaster, which stood 30 feet high and had human faces – 80 chambers, halls, anterooms and apartments adorned with the sculptures, carvings and bronzeware for which Nineveh had by then become famous. The king called it "The Palace without Rival," an assessment no one has contradicted in two and a half thousand years.

But the city – its wealth guaranteed by tribute from the traders who passed through – was a vulnerable citadel and its rulers were fiercely protective, as the presence of such massive, defensive city walls, suggests. The Assyrians were territorial, not to mention warlike and expansionist, and they were brutal conquerors. Their armies were feared and hated throughout the age of their dominance, and when finally Nineveh's time came to an end, there were few who mourned her passing – indeed, as the Bible tells, there was much rejoicing that the Assyrians had finally got their due.

Jonah's God-given task was to stave off the grisly end that finally did befall Nineveh. God saw the city and her people as many of her subjects did: greedy, slothful, ignorant, warlike and godless. But, deciding to give the Ninevens a chance at redemption, He told Jonah to go to the city and remind the people of their pious duties, and tell them that if they did not change their sinful ways, they would be punished. Jonah's opinion of Nineveh conformed with the popular view, and he would have preferred to see the city left to the sorry fate of divine destruction. So he tried to engineer it that way by defying God's direction and buying passage on a ship travelling in the other direction. But God was not to be thwarted: He sent a storm so fierce that all aboard the ship were sure that it would capsize and they would be drowned. So when Jonah told the captain that God had sent the storm because he was disobeying divine direction, the crew threw him overboard. The storm immediately passed, the ship was saved, and a passing whale swallowed Jonah. For three days and nights Jonah sat in the belly of the whale praying for forgiveness for his disobedience and deliverance from what he believed was to be a certain death. When he was finally spat by the whale on to a beach, Jonah had learned his lesson and set out for Nineveh according to his original orders. Once there, he was to warn the residents that they had 40 days and nights to heed their duty to God or they would be destroyed. As Jonah tells it, every man, woman and child, from the king in his palace to the lowliest labourers on the streets, wore sackcloth and ashes, and forswore food and drink for the allotted time to win back God's grace. Which, much to Jonah's chagrin, they did. Seeing Jonah angry that Nineveh had been spared, God explained that the people of the city had risen to the challenge, that given a chance they had done the right thing: heeded the warning and mended their ways.

Sennacherib's son Esarhaddon, who was later to conquer Egypt, built a shrine to Jonah to show the city's thanks to God for sparing the Assyrian capital – at least until the Babylonians laid siege, attacked and razed it in 612 BC.

That shrine, Nebi Yunus, is today one of Mosul's most famous landmarks and is certainly its most important historic religious site. It stands on the east bank of the Tigris, as had Nineveh, opposite the city which was eventually rebuilt on the west bank and named Mosul. Having started life as an Assyrian temple, Nebi Yunus has been at various times a Zoroastrian temple, a monastery, a church and is today a mosque. Jonah's shrine is in a specially built room within the mosque, and on the wall are bones said to be those of the whale that swallowed him whole and spat him out for a second chance at warning the city of encroaching doom. For more than two thousand years, Nebi Yunus has been a focal point for pilgrims from a variety of religions and practices, and though it has been renovated, decorated, embellished and had electricity and plumbing installed, it has never been thoroughly excavated; a winged statue that stands near Jonah's shrine is said to have been found while the mosque was being restored during the late 1980s.

City of God

Mosque, church, monastery, temple and shrine – the layers of Nebi Yunus reflect the religious, cultural and ethnic make-up of the city it shimmers above. After the collapse of the Assyrian empire, King Nebuchadnezzar ruled the region from Babylon, near modern-day Baghdad, and Nineveh's star waned until Mosul rose on the opposite bank of the Tigris in the eighth century AD, becoming a vital pivot for caravan trade along the river, linking Syria and Anatolia via Mesopotamia with India and Persia. Cotton became a principal crop, thriving on the abundant water that ran from the mountain tops, and the plain cloth developed by the local weavers took a name derived from that of the city: muslin. The city managed to maintain a low profile throughout the invasions and occupations that came and went over the centuries – Babylonians, Greeks, Persians (twice) – until 1258, when the Mongol hordes under Hulagu Khan, grandson of Genghis, brother of Kublai, swept through the Orient, destroying any city that did not submit and leaving little behind besides butchered bodies and burning buildings. Saddam Hussein cleverly invoked the carnage and waste of the Mongol invasion when it was clear, in early 2003, that the Americans and British were intent on invading his domain, calling on Iraqis to stand together against the "new Mongols." It was an image of siege and slaughter which had a profound resonance among Iraqi people.

Mesopotamia, which covered an area roughly the same as modern-day Iraq, has been variously fought over, ruled and occupied down the centuries, but it was the rise of the Turkish Ottoman empire which brought revival to Mosul, and once again the city became a centre of political, economic, cultural and religious influence. The Ottomans divided Iraq into three administrative regions, or vilayets – Baghdad, Basra and Mosul –

and the city of Mosul became the capital of Mosul province. Borders as we know them today were not an issue for the farmers, craftsmen and traders of the Ottoman empire, and Mosul became such an important producer and exporter of sheep products – wool, skin, hides – that, it is said, the markets of Aleppo relied almost entirely on produce from Mosul. The city imported yarn and dye, and exported fabrics. Grain from Mosul was vital to the Baghdad and Basra regions during times of southern drought. After centuries of commercial expansion that under the Ottomans had seen Mosul develop into a multilayered social and economic nexus, the trading supremacy of the area was eclipsed somewhat with the opening in 1869 of the Suez Canal. The canal immediately became the principal route of trade between Asia and Europe, joining the Mediterranean to the Red Sea and doing away with the need to circumnavigate Africa. Trade traffic that had for millennia crossed overland through what were now Ottoman lands was willingly diverted as the trip could now be made in record time. For the next half-century, Mosul was once again on the sidelines of the international economy. Until, that is, the discovery of oil in the early twentieth century.

By this time the Ottoman empire had begun to atrophy and its weaknesses were easily exploited by the European powers hungry for the oil they sensed would be vital to fuel their expansionist ambitions. The British, in particular, saw Iraq as a road to India and a buffer to Russia, and its oil as the lifeblood of continued empire. The Ottomans granted concessions for the exploration and control of oil resources throughout Mesopotamia, but once World War I broke out the British captured the three regions of Baghdad, Basra and Mosul. By then Kuwait was a British protectorate and secret deals had been done between the British and the French on a carve-up once the Ottoman empire collapsed, as it did with the end of the war. The French later traded Mosul for oil revenues and territorial guarantees in eastern Syria. Turkey, under the republican and secular Mustafa Kemal Atatürk, continued to claim that Mosul fell within its newly defined borders, tussling with the British until the "Mosul question" was settled in 1925 by a commission of investigators from the League of Nations who found that, by and large, the people preferred to remain under British control. Not long after, just north of Mosul near the town of Kirkuk, British engineers struck one of the biggest oil deposits on the planet.

Mosul was then, like much of northern Iraq, predominantly Kurdish with large numbers of Christians – more than any other city in Iraq, as it had been the centre of Nestorian Christianity and was later important to Chaldean Catholics. Nestorians were followers of Nestorius, Bishop of Constantinople, who had broken with mainstream Christian theology in the fifth century in a dispute over the nature of Christ: god or man (both, he said; god, said those who set doctrinal law). In the sixteenth century, a group of Nestorians aligned themselves with the Vatican and became known as Chaldeans. This colourful history has left the city with many old churches and monasteries that down the ages have performed a sacred duty for these Christian sects. The Mosul region was home to followers of other beliefs, too, including a large number of Jews and the Lucifer-worshipping Yezidis.

During the final years of the Ottoman empire, Mosul became a haven of intrigue as the Christian communities were used as diplomatic pawns by the European powers in strategies aimed at securing leverage over Constantinople that were largely divisive and left an enduring legacy of both religious and ethnic mistrust. The Catholic French and the British, with the help of their missionaries, played various sects off against each other in the larger diplomatic game of expanding their competing political and territorial interests. As in other areas of the Middle East, Iraq's Christians have suffered intermittent persecution and in the fractious sectarian environment that has prevailed in recent years are often targets of violent attacks premised on them selling alcohol, allowing their women broader freedoms than some Muslim groups, cooperating with the occupiers, or simply being Christians.

City of oil

As the Nestorian dominance faded over the ages into Kurdish ascendancy, so the British and their unabashed rush for control of the region's vast oil reserves rapidly buried the political dominance of the Ottomans. The Ottomans had, over the centuries, slipped into the inevitable malaise that comes with long uninterrupted power, and they lost touch with the ways of the world. By the turn of the twentieth century they had little grasp of how things were changing. They believed, for instance, that the territories sitting on the outer reaches of their empire were little more than dusty, irrelevant, poverty-stricken sheikhdoms that would never amount to much and which they could easily do without. The British, and other Western powers, however, understood only too well what places like Iraq, Kuwait and Qatar had to offer. They knew, too, that to consolidate their international power base and build on it, they needed to leave behind the filthy and expensive coal that had fired their industrial birth and switch to oil. Oil, they believed beyond question, was to be had in the Middle East.

With the Mosul question settled, the Turkish Petroleum Company, a British-dominated partnership with French, German, Dutch and American interests, set about the exploration and exploitation of the vast oil reserves of Iraq and her neighbours. The partners wrangled over concessions, cajoled governments of the Middle East into submission, expanded oil production throughout Iraq, including Mosul, and created some of the biggest companies in the world. These firms controlled not only the oilfields and the methods of getting the oil to the surface, but also the means of refining it, and transporting the final product, via pipelines, trucks and ships, to the growing markets in their home countries. As the world's reliance on oil grew, so did the profits of these companies and the protection they enjoyed from their governments. Eventually, the companies' interests became closely and inextricably entwined with the national good.

By the middle of the twentieth century, national good had also become national security, and the dominance and division of the Middle Eastern oilfields became key points of discussion and negotiation between the leaders of Britain and the United States, Prime Minister Winston Churchill and President Franklin Roosevelt, during World War II. A few decades later, President Jimmy Carter set up the US military's Central

Command (or CentCom) specifically as a rapid deployment force that could intervene in the Middle East at short notice, with one of its stated functions to ensure the flow of oil to its international markets. Certainly, there are many analysts who view the modern structure of the United States' armed forces as being primarily focused on ensuring the flow of oil towards the home country's shores in the event of instability anywhere it is produced. The subterfuge and intrigue that accompanied the diplomatic and corporate wrangling over oil rights in the early twentieth century led directly to the involvement of governments and their secret services in the internal political machinations of those countries that held vast reserves of oil.

In the first half of the twentieth century, it was the British who sent their armed forces into Iraq to defend oil resources: during the colonial conquest of 1914–18, when Mosul was first captured; in the long War of Pacification from 1918 to 1930, when Britain used, among other things, chemical weapons – something Churchill said he saw no problem with – to suppress uprisings and insurgents against the British presence in their country; the reoccupation in 1941, which came after Britain through the League of Nations had granted Iraq independence in 1932. As World War II progressed, Britain was desperate that the Axis powers should not encroach on Iraq, and that the United States shouldn't follow through on any designs it might have had on Iraqi oil. So Britain unilaterally took control of Iraq once more. The post-war rise of Arab nationalism provided another challenge to Western control of Iraq's oil, and fears of a challenge to that dominance fuelled early support of the rise of the Ba'ath Party in general and, in particular, of Saddam Hussein. It was with Western support that Saddam was able to play a key role in the attempted assassination, in 1959, of Prime Minister Abd el-Karim Ali, whose pan-Arabist tendencies were feared in Washington and London as a potential threat to the flow of oil.

City of Saddam

With the rise of the Ba'ath Party and Saddam Hussein in the late 1960s and 1970s, oil remained a focal point of his brand of Arab nationalism, directly affecting Mosul, the renamed Ninawa province of which it is capital, and the ethnic and religious demographic balance across northern Iraq. The policy of "Arabization" that Saddam introduced saw tens of thousands of Kurdish people forced off their land and out of their homes, with little or no compensation and rarely the offer of somewhere else to go, replaced by Arabs who were moved up from the south to the northern, largely Kurdish areas. In this way, Saddam hoped to quell Kurdish dissatisfaction with his regime as well as ensure control over the Kirkuk oilfields. Mosul's Arab population grew from what had been a sizeable minority to a majority and Ninawa seethed with barely repressed ethnic tension and resentment that exploded when the Ba'ath Party's brutal government ended with the Allied invasion of 2003.

In 1980, Saddam set his armies against Iran in a war that lasted eight years, claimed around a million lives and was used as a backdrop for the acceleration of Ba'athist nationalism in which Saddam attempted to create and impose a modern Mesopotamian identity on Iraqis that would override the religious and cultural differences of old, and in which he saw threats to his power base. Foreign residents were forced either to take Iraqi citizenship or leave the country; Kurdish was dropped as a medium of education and communication; and the use of English in schools and universities was also banned in favour of Arabic. Men of all ages were drafted to the front in rotation as well as pressed into the service of a "people's army" to provide localized security against the enemy; ordinary citizens were cajoled into giving up their gold and cash to support the war effort. The Western powers once again became involved on the Iraqi side as international support divided along cold war lines, with Russia and China on Iran's side – providing diplomatic back-up, cash and arms to sustain a war that destroyed much of the oil infrastructure of both countries.

With barely enough time to recover from the war against Iran, in 1990

Saddam Hussein's armies annexed Kuwait to make good on a historic and popular claim to the country as an Iraqi province. A few months later, in early 1991, the country was bombed and invaded by a US-led coalition, with the approval of the United Nations. As the Western powers rushed in to secure Kuwaiti oil, Saddam's retreating forces torched hundreds of the nodding donkeys that had placidly marked out the location of some of the world's most productive oil wells.

Kurds across the country's north attempted an uprising against the Ba'athist government, but without the implied support of the United States they hadn't a hope against the Iraqi army, which launched air strikes and chemical weapons attacks against them. In the face of such severe suppression, they fled in huge numbers, in any way they could, across Iraq's borders into Iran, Syria and Turkey. To stem the flow of refugees, Allied warplanes, using bases in southern Turkey, began patrolling "no-fly zones" that were off-limits to the Iraqi military and carrying out bombing sorties across northern Iraq – and also in the south, where similar uprisings had been attempted by Shia Muslims. Kurdish militia-backed political parties were able to delineate what became a quasi-independent Kurdish administrative zone within a "line of control" which Saddam's forces were not permitted to cross. Mosul was outside this line of control but within the no-fly zone. So while Saddam's forces were unable to do much more than fire half-hearted missile volleys at the patrolling American and British fighter jets, they were able to recruit large numbers of men from within the city to the ranks of the Fifth Army, which was garrisoned there, and to continue the "Arabization" of the city and surrounding areas that changed the ethnic face of Ninawa province. From 1991 and for the next twelve years, the deprivations suffered by Iraqi people intensified amid a programme of international sanctions backed by a low-intensity war against Saddam's regime. A handful of major attacks were launched by the American and British air forces from the Turkish bases, destroying some military infrastructure in and around Mosul and other areas, and killing many civilians as well. The oil-for-food programme instituted by the United Nations was a shambles, with the corrupt benefiting as ordinary people could no longer afford to buy simple foodstuffs such as milk, and hospitals going without basic medicines. Unable to rebuild much of the infrastructure that had been destroyed in the Iran–Iraq War, Iraq slipped into Third World levels of poverty, with people of all classes forced to line up for monthly rations of everything from soap to flour. The oil wealth of the nation remained mostly underground, as the trade blockade and the aggressive patrolling of the no-fly zones kept other potential partners, French and Russians among them, eager to help rebuild and get the fuel flowing once more, on the nervous sidelines.

The terrorist attacks on the United States on September 11, 2001, provided the administration of President George W. Bush and his senior advisers – many of them former executives of the American oil and related industries – with a pretext for invading Iraq and toppling Saddam Hussein's regime that has since been largely discredited. Contrary to Allied claims, Saddam did not have any link to the terrorist network of Osama bin Laden's Al Qaeda, nor had he stockpiles of biological, chemical and nuclear weapons of mass destruction that could be used to attack British and American interests inside an hour, as the British government claimed. Britain's cooperation with the American project should have come as no surprise when seen in the context of its historic involvement in the oil industry of Iraq. Saddam himself saw it coming, and by the time of the Allied invasion of Iraq in the Second Gulf War, in March, 2003, Mosul was seething as the line of control – already a front line over which the Iraqi army took regular potshots at villagers on the other side – had become the front line of what was expected to be the "northern front" of the war to topple the Ba'athist government. Intelligence at the time estimated the troop strength in the city at 80,000, backed by tanks and other armoury. While the northern front did not take the shape originally intended – because Turkey would not allow its southern bases to be used to pursue a war that did not have the approval of the United Nations – American forces were airdropped in and set up bases in Iraqi Kurdistan. With the cooperation and local knowledge of the Kurdish peshmerga militiamen, the Americans engaged the Iraqis in some fierce fighting, calling in air strikes on specific targets along and behind the line of control. The city fell on April 11, two days after Baghdad. The Iraqi army disappeared, and thousands of tonnes of ammunition and arms were left in barracks and in dumps across the countryside to be looted by what would become the guerrilla war of resistance to the occupation, which, it now appears, was planned well in advance of the Allied invasion. In the meantime, gangs of Kurds rampaged across the line of control on vigilante missions throughout Ninawa and Mosul to reclaim land and homes that had been taken from them.

In the days after the fall of the Ba'ath Party and the disappearance of Saddam Hussein, Nebi Yunus played a prominent role in Mosul's infamously active rumour mill. The story went that the night before Mosul fell, a convoy of 35 white stretch limousines had pulled up at the steps outside Nebi Yunus. As the engines of the sleek, imported, black-windowed vehicles idled, and moonlight glinted off their flawlessly polished coachwork, a solitary figure emerged to climb the steps into the old Nestorian sandstone building. Soon after, his prayers done, the tall, moustachioed, round-bellied man in army fatigues climbed back into his car, and the convoy sped off to the north-west, towards the Syrian border. That, according to Mosul legend, was how Saddam Hussein made his escape.

Three months later, Mosul was the scene of a vicious firefight when the Americans were tipped off that Saddam's horrendous sons, Uday and Qusay, were hiding out in the city's suburbs. Both were killed and their bullet-ravaged bodies displayed to the local and international media to provide proof to the Iraqi people that the return of the dynasty that had veiled their country in terror and repression for decades was no longer something to be feared. And then, in early December, 2003, Saddam himself was shown on television being dragged out of a hole in the ground by American soldiers near his home town of Tikrit. "We got him," L. Paul Bremer III, head of the occupying Coalition Provisional Authority, told a press conference. Saddam's era was officially over.

City of occupation

The trouble in and around Mosul that followed the war escalated as a complex array of factors continued to play themselves out in the new freedom that had been swept in with the official end of the Ba'athist regime. Guerrilla warfare against the occupation had begun on the day of the city's liberation from Saddam, as soldiers had disappeared from view but not from active duty. Factions began to emerge within the so-called resistance, some of them dividing, inevitably, along sectarian lines, others emerging simply as gangs bent on exploiting local people for profit. Attacks against locals working with the Americans deterred many from joining the police and army, and so the job of maintaining what passed for law and order fell mainly to the peshmerga. With the bitter memory of the Kurdish vigilantes still clear in the minds of many, the presence in the city of ethnic militia working with the US forces just confirmed many in their suspicions that the Americans were on the Kurds' side in the ongoing property and land disputes. In order to bring some objective and stable policing to the streets of Mosul, the Kurds were replaced with local Arabs in an attempt to rebuild a trustworthy and effective police force. This backfired when, as the US army was attempting to clear Fallujah, a resistance stronghold to the south of Mosul, of anti-occupation insurgents, the Mosul police force handed control of their city to those guerrillas who were said to be moving out of Fallujah and coming farther north to escape the American bombardment. Senior police officers were sacked, Kurds were re-employed and the two sides fought in the streets, often with tragic consequences for innocent people caught in the crossfire.

As the city slid into anarchy and violence, US bases were attacked by snipers and suicide bombers; car bombs were regularly set off throughout the commercial district as well as at US bases and, later, recruiting centres for the army and police; gangs patrolled neighbourhoods demanding protection money from shopkeepers and professionals; supplies of electricity and water were intermittent at best; and the price and availability of fuel for cooking and heating skyrocketed. Internet and mobile phone services became increasingly unreliable as the city sank farther out of reasonable control and into the criminal maw of terrorism. People who could get out began doing so by any means. To stay was to court danger and death.

Even amid the initial anarchy and looting that followed the fall of the Ba'ath, an early hope had prevailed in Mosul. In the first few days and weeks after the city's liberation, most people wanted to believe the violence to be an aberration. Law and order were not far away, they said, trying to believe that the occupiers would bring stability, security and jobs, that the mistrust and lies and oppression of the Saddam epoch were gone for good, that soon everything would be normal. But as time and violence dragged on, hope faded until, like a burned-out candle, faith in the future flickered into a melancholy darkness, replaced by a selfish desperation simply to survive.

The intersection by Nebi Yunus is known as "Kurdish Corner," a gathering point for Kurdish day labourers who came to Mosul looking for casual work – digging, building, repairing, hauling. Contractors who could paint a room, fix a roof, dig over a bed of gardenias, put up a garage and retile a bathroom came to Nebi Yunus to offer their skills to residents who came in turn to haggle over the conditions and cost. In a city of almost 2 million, there was always work to be found. For householders, the prices were competitive, and for the Kurdish contractors, the income steady. By early 2006, however, few in Mosul were spending money on house repairs, or even new clothes, fearful of any display of wealth, and the Kurds stopped coming.

Everyone stopped coming. Jonah's shrine was no longer a destination for thanksgiving pilgrimages by people from across the sectarian spectrum. But having withstood more than two thousand years of war and occupation, and the misery they bring, its presence on al-Tawba Hill overlooking Mosul from the opposite bank of the Tigris attests to the constancy of human resilience and the ability of people to rebuild their lives once the lunacy and violence have passed.

5

Building Strength and Character

Pauline Basheer and Margaret al-Sharook, the Englishwomen of Mosul, have taken many parallel paths through their lives, from northern England to northern Iraq. Their friendship endured through the hardships and deprivations of almost thirty years of war in what began as an alien land and became the only home they knew or wanted. It would be easy to think of them as being more similar than not. But the ways in which their paths diverged, and the contrasts in their characters shaped by those differences, are as stark as sunshine and shadow.

Margaret often shows the intense reserve of one who has learned to keep her own counsel under stringent social and political constraints. Pauline, of course, also displays the caution that is essential for survival in a country controlled by a paranoid dictator. She does not seem to have absorbed this reticence into her approach to thought and expression, unlike Margaret, who in talking to me about her life often fudged or left out details in order, I believe, to protect the image of her family. Pauline was an open book, leaving nothing out, unashamed of her emotions and her reactions to what was an often difficult life with Ali. Margaret's instinct was restraint, which could often stretch towards obfuscation when it came to how her husband's membership of the Ba'ath Party influenced events in her life. Politics were inescapable in Iraq and loomed over every aspect of life, for every person, regardless of their station. For Margaret, the politics of Saddam's Iraq were even closer than they were for most people because of who her husband was, and so had a greater direct influence on her quality of life than she is, perhaps, willing to concede.

In our many conversations, there were always contradictory currents. Margaret stressed her role as traditional wife and mother, uninterested in, and even ignorant of, political and social developments outside her family. But it did become clear over time that she was very much aware that the status and comfort that accumulated as her husband's career progressed were due – not uniquely, but certainly in large part – to his closeness to Saddam's regime.

The outstanding difference in the lives of the two women in the decades leading up to the 2003 Allied invasion was their relationship to the prevailing system of government. Margaret married a man who had a stake in political continuity; Pauline's husband was determinedly apolitical. Each of the women wears a protective layer that, like nacre covering a grain of sand that has infiltrated an oyster shell, thickened over time and of necessity in the brutal and brutalizing atmosphere of the Iraq they lived in. Yet the nature of the camouflage each wears is peculiar to their contrasting circumstances.

Iraq is a country where what you know is often simply a back-up for who you know. Zuhair was a talented and conscientious careerist who, in Margaret's words, "worked 24-7," and would often hardly be seen at home for days if he was busy at the university – where he rose through the academic and bureaucratic ranks to become president. Sometimes he was away for weeks and even months if he was on assignment elsewhere in Iraq or abroad, taking courses and recruiting faculty in Europe, India and South Asia, and neighbouring Middle Eastern countries. The rewards for such dedication, in most countries, are promotion and privilege. In Iraq, for partisans and promoters of the government agenda, these rewards rarely came in the form of salary rises, but were mostly paid in kind – besides the occasional cash bonus there was access to cars and, sometimes, chauffeurs; family vacations at party resorts; parcels of land both in the city, on which to build the family's principal home, and in rural areas for holiday getaways. With a large household to run, Margaret and Zuhair were by no means rich, and during the difficult times of Saddam's tenure they faced the same hardships as most Iraqis – and the same restrictions on having overseas bank accounts and holding foreign passports. Zuhair's position and loyalty to the Iraqi state, however, brought his family prestige and privilege.

There is no question that Zuhair was fiercely patriotic, a nationalist who had bought into the Ba'athist agenda in which all power flowed to, and from, the state. The party had been formed in Syria in the 1940s, advocating a single Arab socialist nation in reaction to the colonialism and imperialism that had dominated centuries of regional politics. It took power in Syria in 1963, and remains the sole party of government there today. In Iraq, its road to dominance was a little rockier, with the party taking but losing government after a coup in 1963, and regaining it in a revolution in 1968. As in many socialist revolutions throughout history, the Ba'ath claimed popular support that was consolidated through a tightening stranglehold on political and intellectual freedom, with all opposition wiped out as dissenters fled the country, were jailed, executed or disappeared. Differences between the Syrian and Iraqi branches of the Ba'ath Party precluded unification of the two countries into a larger Arab state, though Saddam Hussein sought to overcome the complex cocktail of ethnic, religious and class differences within Iraq to build the country into a centrally controlled, secular, Arab state. Oil was pivotal to Ba'athist power, and the nationalization of the industry ensured that the country grew rich and comfortable even as Iraq was rivalling the Soviet Union, China and other one-party states in its cruelty and tyranny. In essence, Saddam used a progressive agenda to stir the country and its varied groups into a mix he could dominate. Zuhair, like many ambitious pragmatists, understood and rode that trend.

Patriotism and loyalty to a tyrant are accompanied by constant strains and scrutiny. Privilege brings vulnerability to the enmity and envy of colleagues and neighbours, and can easily be derailed by incautious words or deeds. The privileged of the totalitarian states of the late twentieth century didn't necessarily live in golden palaces. Rather, in lands of scarcity, favours that could seem to Western eyes unimportant or even tedious had a life-changing significance to people denied basic freedoms. Attendance at a conference abroad, for instance, meant a hard currency per diem that could buy goods, such as washing machines or colour televisions or French perfume, that were not available at home. Or American cigarettes that could be used to smooth the wheels of a Byzantine bureaucracy. These perks were status symbols for the lucky few, as well as the pay-off for their fealty.

For many people who live within the strictures of totalitarianism, it can be a shock that these conditions do not apply to governments everywhere, and that in normal countries people are generally free to think and believe, and speak and act, as they wish. On the only occasion that I met Zuhair, he told me that he did not want anything to appear in print that would reveal details of his allegiance to Saddam's Iraq, fearing it might jeopardize his chances of being granted a visa to resettle permanently in Britain. He told me carefully and in allusions, trying not to make it too clear, in case I didn't know, that he had been a senior party member and thus might be regarded as an enemy by the governments that had engineered the invasion of his country and, thereby, the ruin of his life. In making his point, at great length, not only did he betray a fundamental lack of understanding of the nature of British society, one of the most liberal and tolerant in western Europe, but an ignorance of the reach of the international mainstream media, which had covered, in detail, the very public way in which he came to leave Iraq in late 2003. He seemed not to understand that, in the West, information is not the exclusive currency of the powerful, as it is in dictatorships and certainly had been in Iraq, where Saddam had implemented a system of surveillance so all-embracing that no one was safe from prying eyes, not even the spies. I suspect that Margaret shared this naivety, as the habits of many years, be they physical or psychological, can be difficult to break.

The wily skill of stalking around a topic in order to glean what is known by the person one is talking to, without adding to their knowledge, was well practised in Zuhair and most likely had made a great contribution to his career trajectory – which was not, incidentally, without the inevitable blips caused by the jealousy and vindictiveness of those around him. He reached the senior party rank of "shuba" but could go no higher, Margaret says, "because he was married to me." His concern with the perceptions of others seems to have infused his family, as at least one of his sons was so eager to preserve the correct image that he would not allow his big sister to appear in public wearing trousers because it was regarded as vulgar. And another son who climbed the ladder of student politics at college inherited his ambitious streak. In Margaret, Zuhair's influence appeared to manifest itself in a taciturn discretion. She told me that she had learned to appear to cooperate with those around her, and say all the right things, while doing what she pleased. "I didn't like it very much, the interfering. They'd always do everything better than you – they could cook better than you, they could bring their children up better than you, and they'd tell you," Margaret remembered. "I'm easy going, so I'd take so much and then not take any more and just ignore it – how the kids should be dressed, why am I not wearing a headscarf. I'd say: 'Because I don't want to.' You become the biggest liar on earth, depending on who you're talking to. Rumours and gossip are rife, part of the culture." Her early decisions to be conservative in her manner of dress, and in her dealings outside the home, were doubtless influenced by Zuhair's need to conform, and perhaps even resulted from a subtle pressure he exerted on Margaret to keep up appearances at all times, and at all costs, in order not to damage his prospects within the party and for career advancement. For in Iraq, for Zuhair, the two were inextricable.

Pauline tells the story of her own epiphany regarding the need for discretion, and political correctness, to devastating effect, and her animation describes the impact of the thunderbolt that struck her with an intensity that has never diminished. It came during a visit with Ali to Baghdad soon after her arrival in Iraq, before babies came along and "while I was still very green," as she put it. Ali had wanted to show off to his new bride the beauty of the legendary capital, and indulge her love of history and of the central role her adopted country had played in the development of civilization. She was terribly excited, not only by the palpable weight of the ages that Baghdad imposes on first-time visitors. She was knocked out to see young Baghdadi women in miniskirts and patent-leather, knee-high boots, their hair teased up, their boyfriends in sharp, modish suits with drainpipe trousers and winkle-picker shoes, taking the girls around on the back of Piaggio-style scooters. She walked through the boulevards and back alleys of Baghdad soaking it all in. Until one afternoon, while out window-shopping with Ali, she made a huge, and potentially damaging, mistake.

"I was looking in a shop window and I saw a watch with Saddam's face on it. I burst out laughing because it was the most ridiculous thing I'd ever seen. Well, Ali grabbed me by the back of the neck," she says, reaching behind her head and yanking her own collar, "and dragged me straight back to the hotel, packed up our things, and dragged me straight back to Mosul. He was that scared!"

She told another story – which might be apocryphal, but then again might not – about a little boy who during the Iran–Iraq War was asked by his teacher at nursery school: "What does Daddy say when he watches TV?"

"The little boy told the teacher: 'He swears about *that man* on the television.' Well, she wasn't a teacher, she was security. So the father had to leave – leave Mosul and leave Iraq," Pauline said. "After that, I knew, and I told the kids never to say anything about Papa Saddam, as he was referred to. We never talked about politics anyway, and didn't take an interest, Ali not being in the party."

Politics just wasn't on the agenda as a topic of conversation for anyone in Iraq who wanted to stay alive, let alone stay out of prison. Any sort of grumble could be taken as an expression of anti-government sentiment, and so it had to be bottled up. For women who came from modern, Western societies where it is a basic ethos to question authority, complain when it falls short of expectations and take action for change, Iraq's authoritarianism and Saddam's reign of terror led to tremendous frustrations and, in some cases among the foreign women who became friends of Pauline and Margaret, to mental breakdown. One of the few ways in which the foreign women in Mosul dealt with this need for a pressure valve was to get together for tea – high tea – while their men were at work and their children at school, and talk. Not about politics, but about whatever small problem was niggling them at that moment – the electricity wasn't working properly; the weather was too hot to sleep; the dust from the desert lay thick on the furniture half an hour after it was dusted;

their mothers-in-law were driving them mad; their husbands insisted the dolma were made to taste exactly the same as those their mums made. The women who sat around the high tea tables of Mosul came from England and Wales, Germany and Ireland, America and Sweden. They complained that they couldn't go shopping by themselves; that their relatives wanted them to wear headscarves; that their husbands were retreating into their religion; that they couldn't find OXO cubes or decent potatoes; that they'd had their bottoms pinched while walking on Nineveh Street; that they were sick to death of mutton, mutton and more mutton. They told stories about their interfering neighbours and the busybody colleagues of their husbands, about the gossips of Mosul who are renowned throughout Iraq for their rumour-mongering and nastiness. They would laugh about their own shortcomings – how their kibbeh (meat pies) always fell apart while being boiled, or how no matter how hard they tried, their rice always turned out like mush. Sometimes they would make cakes, whatever was their speciality (Margaret was known for her sensational custard butter cream cake, another for her currant slices, another for her biscuits, still another for her doughnuts), and they'd brew pot after pot of tea while they bellyached, and moaned, and gossiped, and laughed. Sometimes they'd get together in groups of four – as Olive, Margaret's mother, did at least once a week with some of the older women – and play Scrabble, drink coffee, smoke cigarettes and reminisce. And at the end of the afternoon, they'd go back to their own homes, in time for the children to come in from school, to get them started on their homework, many – including Pauline and, later, Margaret – to look after their mothers-in-law, and to begin the evening bustle about the kitchen, knowing that no matter how tough things got or how lonely they sometimes felt, they weren't alone; they had friends who saw things the same way they did, who would look out for them, who loved them. And so, for a little while every now and then at least, the burden of being a foreign wife in Iraq had been eased, and everything felt better.

Margaret threw herself into family life, and into the high-status role as wife of the oldest son of an established, well-off Mosul merchant family. She had landed in the labyrinth of old Mosul and immediately fallen in love with the place. "Olde worlde," she called it. "It was all houses close together, narrow alleyways; very, very old. It wasn't leafy or green; there were no trees because the houses were so close together. People – well, the men – would sit out on their doorsteps, like in England in the old days. Everyone knew everyone else, and their business, and you didn't need to lock your doors. Time moved very slowly. It was a lazy type of life."

These *mahalle*, as the old neighbourhoods are called, grew up over time and by the turn of the nineteenth century the core of the old city was made up of 34 distinct precincts with mosques, madrasas (religious schools), public baths and civic spaces for prayer. Many have bustling piazzas where farmers set up stalls in the mornings to sell produce, and there are small shops selling everything from toothpaste to cotton socks. There are sitting-out areas for, mostly, the men. The Tigris was just a few minutes' walk from Margaret's front door, handy for a stroll once the heat had gone out of the day. The banks of the Tigris were a natural play-ground, and as Margaret's children grew up, the river became a swimming hole for her three boys. "I used to think how nice it would be if I could go for a swim," she said. Of course, she couldn't; that was a public pastime for men only. But like everything that was imposed on her by the local culture, "you just get used to it."

The place was "normal" in those days, she said, remembering the girls' miniskirts and bare arms. Religion was not a factor until a few years later – during the Iran–Iraq War when Saddam tried to impose piety as a way of justifying a hopeless venture that wasted millions of lives and billions of dollars. Then the headscarves started appearing and Saddam had "God is great" – *Allahu Akhbar* – added to the national flag in his own hand. When Margaret arrived, however, just before that war began, Iraq was secular and socialist, the people were educated and literate, and 95 per cent of all girls went to school, up from fewer than 30 per cent a decade earlier. But it's the tribalism and traditions which die hardest and, as Margaret said, as a woman "you lose your identity in Arabic culture.

Of course, Zuhair being well known, I got respect through him. I was 'wife of Zuhair,' 'mother of Ali.' People would ask, who is your husband? Where does he work? I didn't mind. It's just the way it is." Not wanting to draw attention to herself – a tall order, as she is blonde and stands at almost six feet – she rarely left the house alone. Her husband says now that she was too cautious in the early days – an easy observation to make with the hindsight of almost thirty years. Margaret says she was escorted everywhere because that's how she wanted things to be, and to be fair it was easier for her than for most people, as often the university provided Zuhair with a car and a driver who would ferry Margaret around town at her convenience.

Margaret found that everyone in Zuhair's family spoke English to varying degrees of fluency and were happy to have a native speaker in their midst with whom they could practise. For a short time, she had an administrative job at Mosul University, where there were so many foreign teachers that the language on campus was English; many of the classes were taught in English, too. So Margaret had to insist to her family that they speak to her in Arabic. She was desperate to know what was going on around her and to be able to participate. Within a couple of years she was competent enough to know all the family and neighbourhood gossip. And as she learned the ways of the Moslawis, she learned, too, what to say and what to keep to herself.

For Moslawis, many people in Iraq will tell you for nothing, have a reputation for minding everyone's business, and embellishing it as they pass it on. Moslawi women are known for their vicious tongues ("They say that if you can deal with a Moslawi woman, you can deal with anyone," a long-time resident of the city told me) and Moslawi men as misers. One native of the city told me that a Moslawi man would rather wear rags and count his money than spend it on new clothes. Others tell of how competitive the women are, attending social occasions to gauge the wealth and standing of their hosts and fellow guests. "At weddings," one Arab Iraqi, another native of the city, told me, "the women will sit there and assess the value of the gold that the bride is wearing, and make judgements about the family she is marrying into based on that. Then they will go and view the things she has received from her own family, and make judgements about the bride's family based just on that. And then they'll tell everyone they know, whether it is true or not." Many times, both Margaret and Pauline told me in the same words, "everyone in Mosul knows everyone else's business." And neither of them seemed to think it was a good thing. Indeed, Pauline said she and Ali didn't attend social functions unless they felt they absolutely had to, and had found that staying at home was an effective way of keeping their business to themselves. "I've met people who didn't even know I'd had children, so I think it worked to some extent," Pauline said. "Of course, you walk a fine line in working out who is going to get a face on if you don't turn up, so some things you have to go to."

I found it surprising that neither Pauline nor Margaret really prepared themselves for their arrival in Iraq. Pauline was tickled to think that she was going to a biblical land of familiar fables, where she could immerse herself in the fairy-tale romance of Scheherazade's *Arabian Nights* and breathe the same air as Ali Baba and Sinbad, Nebuchadnezzar and Tamerlane, and once she was settled she read and absorbed whatever knowledge she could. Today she still talks about the architecture, crafts, traditions and customs of Mosul with the enthusiasm of a newcomer. Margaret said she didn't read one book about Iraq before she got there. "I probably should have," she added, laughing. "But it probably wouldn't have made a difference. I had heard different stories from people who had lived in Iraq, and travelled to Iraq, things about the heat, for instance. But not much beyond that." She didn't read about Iraq after arriving either, she said. "I was living it." Neither of them knew much about the current politics of the place when it became their home, or its progression through Ottoman to British rule, from kingdom to republic to dictatorship. And neither seems to have taken a great interest in the broader political developments that took place during their early time in Iraq, more naturally focusing on the immediate aggravations, such as food shortages during times of war and international embargoes, or, when hatred of the West was the order of the day, whether their half-English children were being bullied at school.

Saddam Hussein had been running the country for about a decade – formally taking over as president in 1979 – when the two English-women arrived in Mosul. His brutality was no secret, though there was no reason for Pauline and Margaret to expect any concomitant infringement upon their day-to-day concerns with setting up house and getting on with married life. But in late 1980 all that changed when Saddam invaded Iran, and suddenly the inhumanity, violence, pointlessness and cruelty of war became the wallpaper of their lives.

"It was on television all the time. I had to stop the kids watching television. It was terrible. All the dead bodies. And you could tell they'd been gassed because they were black. No bullet holes. And not just one or two, but piles of them. Iranians. Showing us the 'great victories,'" all delivered by a screaming anchorman, said Pauline. Judging by the huge numbers of people who in the early couple of years after war was declared spent their evenings by the river, or in the parks, or strolling along Nineveh Street, or enjoying the rides at the amusement fair, not many stayed home to watch TV. Pretty soon, shops began selling videotape recorders, in defiance of Iraqi law – which also banned ownership of photocopiers, fax machines, cameras and computers without written permission – and then video cassettes of movies. Who wanted to watch a five-hour speech by the president if they could get hold of pirated movies and have a night in watching Jennifer Beals in *Flashdance* or Arnold Schwarzenegger as the Terminator?

The armies of the two neighbours pounded each other for shifting control of tiny slivers of territory, but very little of the action came to Mosul. "We didn't see very much of it – now and again you'd hear that the poorer areas of the city had been hit by missiles, and one morning at about seven a.m. two Iranian planes flew over and there was a lot of anti-aircraft fire. There was word that they'd dropped two bombs in the river to contaminate the water, so there was a bit of panic for a couple of days. But it soon died down," Pauline said.

There were occasional shortages of sugar, tea, powdered milk for babies and soap powder, and there were fights in the local shops when word went around the housing estates that supplies had arrived. Buses would turn up at the university gates to take students, often against their will, into the centre of town to perform in anti-Iran, pro-Saddam rallies staged for the television cameras. Government agents would tour the suburbs pressuring men to join up – effectively press-ganging, as once they'd been asked to volunteer, the men could hardly refuse. Celebrities were regularly shown on television donating their savings and gold jewellery to the war effort, each appearance signalling a renewed campaign for funds as the government's ability to pay for the ongoing war diminished.

Mostly, though, for the people of Iraq, the war was death, and death was all around them, all the time. Death wrapped itself in black and hung off every house, in every corner, every shop and every mosque. Death flags festooned Jonah's shrine at Nebi Yunus, with the names and ranks of the dead who had been washed at the mosque there, and directions to the non-stop funerals where the wailing of mourners intermingled with radio broadcasts from Iran. The people constantly tuned into Iranian radio in the hope of hearing their loved ones' names among the lists of prisoners of war that were broadcast daily. PoW meant alive. Not dead. Mothers and wives travelled alone to the death fields of Basra, touring the battlefields or scouring the hospitals, tormenting officers and doctors in the hope of finding the sons and husbands whose letters had abruptly stopped weeks, months or even years before. More often than not, the women returned home to Mosul alone, with no word of the fate of their men, and no body. The depression of death became the mood of Mosul, the funeral feast its only celebration. No family was untouched.

In 1981, not long after Pauline returned to Mosul, with her baby daughter Noor, who was born in Lancashire in late 1980, she and Ali drove to Gerver, his home village, for the funeral of a cousin who had died on the road near the Basra battlefield. The spectacle of the funeral was as shocking as news of the young man's death. Certainly the memory of the age-old rituals followed by the women of Ali's tribe, which predate Islam in the Kurdish mountains of Ninawa province, is burned on to Pauline's heart, and as she recalls it, a quarter of a century later, and shares it, her breath quickens, tears swim in her eyes, and she is convinced that there is no telling that will do justice to the raw wretchedness she witnessed. The Gerver women, who traditionally wear their hair in long plaits that they coil around their heads, first cut off their pigtails to display their grief. Then they scratched their faces, shredding the skin of their cheeks until blood coursed down their necks. They stood in a circle and crossed their arms over their chests and swayed from side to side. With each sway they beat their chests with their fists, uncrossing their arms and crossing them again, alternating left over right, right over left as they swayed, each time beating their clenched fists against their chests harder and harder. Working themselves into a collective trance of agonized sorrow, the women wailed and cried and screamed and sang prayers. Over and over, inconsolably and incessantly. Not for the usual three days and nights but, because the man who died was the head of his family, for seven days and nights. "It was terrible," Pauline said as she pressed her lips together to control the emotion that had been dredged to the surface by the memory. "I don't think that unless you witness it, you can imagine what it is like; it claws at your soul."

As war, loss and mourning became a way of life in Mosul, Margaret and Zuhair decided to pack up and leave. Zuhair had accepted a position at a university in Algeria – lecturing in biology at the University of Algiers, where he was able to earn more than he would have in Mosul at the time and so could save, relatively quickly, enough money to build a house on the land he'd been granted upon his return from Britain. The land was on an estate that belonged to Mosul University. Land grants were just one of the perks that Saddam Hussein's government used to lure scholarship students back from their overseas studies so they could put their knowledge and skills to use in the service of the modern, pan-Arab, Ba'athist state that he was building. Another was permission to import a new car, tax free, so Zuhair had bought himself a Mercedes – the car in which he ferried

Margaret home to Mosul across Europe and Turkey. By the time they left for Algiers, Margaret had settled into Mosul life, comfortably ensconced as a member of the extended al-Sharook family. Any fears Zuhair had that she might feel alienated and decide, as some of the other Western wives had, to go home had dissolved as Margaret was, she said, happy from the very first day. She'd also given birth, in 1979, to their daughter, Alia – though the child's arrival prompted one of the elderly al-Sharook aunts to declare Margaret "only good for girls," an ominous and damning declaration in the misogynist Arab world of the 1970s (or even today). But pretty soon after they'd settled in Algiers, along came twins Ali and Omar, and then – by accident, Margaret said, laughing – Taleb. Proving the aunt mistaken was one thing; coping with four babies aged under three was another. But help had descended on Margaret's tiny fifth-floor flat in a university compound overlooking a squatters' camp in the sprawling Algerian capital in the towering form of her mother, Olive, who swapped her quiet life of semi-retirement in Durham for the hectic tasks of "chief cook and bottle washer," as she called herself, to Margaret's unruly brood. Olive came back with Margaret to Algiers in 1981, after the birth of the twins in Newcastle. Margaret had been advised by the British embassy to have her babies in England because hospital hygiene in Algeria left a lot to be desired. She was, unfortunately, to find that out for herself within the year when she contracted hepatitis while pregnant with Taleb and had to spend months in an Algiers hospital. She'd lie awake at night watching the cockroaches that had colonized her bedside cabinet, and had to go home each Saturday for her only bath of the week.

The al-Sharook family's stint in Algeria was interrupted in mid-1982, when Margaret and the children followed Zuhair back to Mosul, staying with her in-laws while he completed his mandatory two months of annual national service in the so-called people's army. This was a civilian militia, officially known as the Popular Army, which was originally established to provide Ba'ath Party cadres with military training so they could protect party interests across the country. By the time of the Iran–Iraq War, it had grown to more than 250,000 men who were conscripted for compulsory service and, though they were ineffective in battle, they were required to guard civilian and government buildings and installations. By the late 1980s the Popular Army had developed as a parallel military force, and though it did send fighting units into battle in the seventies and eighties, its primary functions were political: educating the masses to be loyal to the Ba'ath Party, and providing a counterbalance in case of a coup within the regular armed forces. By the late eighties, the Popular Army was supplementing the regular army of 1 million with an additional 650,000 trained men. The Popular Army was ultimately disbanded, in the mid- to late nineties, though men – including students and teachers at schools, colleges and universities – were expected to "volunteer" for military training that could occupy them for up to four hours a day. Each household was expected to have at least one volunteer. At the time of Operation Iraqi Freedom in 2003, the head of every household in Mosul was believed to possess a rifle and was trained to use it in defence of the city in the event of an invasion by the "new Mongols."

In 1983, well before they had planned to return to Mosul, Margaret and Zuhair heard from home that one of his younger brothers, Thamir, was ill, having suffered a recurrence of leukaemia. Thamir had been particularly close to both of them, and had overseen the start of work on their new house, having the architectural plans drawn up to Margaret's specifications and making sure that construction was proceeding according to schedule and cost. The family had believed, hoped, that his remission would be permanent, but as his condition gradually worsened, Thamir decided he wanted to follow in the footsteps of an acquaintance who had also had leukaemia and had undergone a successful bone marrow transplant in London. Zuhair and Margaret returned to Mosul from Algiers, and, as it turned out, Zuhair was found to be compatible as a donor for Thamir. So he and Thamir and Olive headed for London.

"I went to Baghdad to see him off and say goodbye," Margaret remembered. "I never saw him again. The operation didn't work and he died. He'd had the transplant, but then he was dehydrated, and his kidneys gave up and he died.

"I rang Zuhair on his birthday, November the 10th, to say happy birthday, and I was shouted at down the phone, because his brother had died two or three days earlier, and he didn't want the family to know yet. It would have been terrible for them, the place would have been chaotic. Zuhair didn't want them to know until absolutely necessary. So he told the men – he rang one of them, and so they knew, and they told one of the older women. Then they came home and told the mam.

"Zuhair had to bring the body home. He flew him back in a coffin. In the couple of days since his brother had died, he'd arranged everything and then flew him home on his birthday. Thamir had to have the operation. His friend who had it lived for another ten years. There was a sixty per cent chance of it working in those days, so he had to try. He would have died anyway, without trying. Everyone put in what they could to cover the cost, of going to London for the operation, and then of getting him back home."

Construction of Margaret and Zuhair's house continued, with the help of a small bank loan, which was also part of the returned students' package, and the proceeds of the sale of the Mercedes. Moving into her new home in 1984 "was like starting anew," Margaret said. "It was beautiful. It had double walls with insulation in between, so it was comfortable in winter and summer. We bought the kitchen in England because they didn't have them in Iraq, only in solid wood or steel. I wanted a proper kitchen. It's still going, that kitchen. It's nice and big. I looked after it. It opens on to a dining room, and has an open breakfast bar. We'd all sit around in the kitchen, around the table, when my girlfriends came over.

"We built extra rooms, too. It had three bedrooms but we had more kids than we planned, and then my mam came. We have a lovely garden with gardenias, and a grill so that if anyone came over, we'd have barbecues. It was always full of people, always kids racing around." The estate, in an area of Mosul near the university called Katafa, was occupied by faculty members, doctors and professors, many of whom, like Zuhair, had brought home wives they had met while studying abroad. "So we all had our new houses, and we'd be in and out of each other's places all the time," she said. "Life was terrific."

The Iran–Iraq War progressed, and Margaret and Pauline watched many of their girlfriends leave, sickened by the tragic waste, gnawed by the constant grief, their Iraqi husbands eager to escape the straitjacket of Ba'athism. Ali's career was progressing and he was increasingly busy. In the mid-eighties, the government eased restrictions and Ali was able to open his own cardiology clinic. He was also working at the coronary care unit at the Mosul Teaching Hospital, of which he was eventually to become head. He lectured in cardiology at Mosul University's medical school, and became the head of that, too. He had beds at the teaching hospital for his own patients, and supervised his students in their internships. In the years before the 2003 invasion, Ali laid the groundwork for Mosul's first, and Iraq's second, coronary catheter clinic, for which he also had to attend courses in Baghdad to learn how to perform angiograms. Work on the clinic was interrupted by the war, but restarted almost immediately afterwards as a high-priority project. When it opened in late 2004, Ali was performing around four angiograms a day. (An angiogram is an X-ray test of the blood flow within an artery, and is performed by inserting a catheter near the groin or elbow, and guiding a tube to the area to be studied; dye is then forced into the vein, so the X-ray shows whether the vein is damaged in any way.) Ali, a slight man whose easy laugh has etched jolly lines around his warm, brown eyes, was well known and respected in Mosul. He rarely refused requests for help and was often left wondering what on earth he was going to do with a sheep that had been left on his step by a patient as payment in kind for his services. ("I could never eat a lamb or sheep that had arrived alive, it would choke me," said Pauline, who believes the halal method of slaughter, in which the beast's throat is cut and it bleeds slowly to death, to be "barbaric" and an example of the cruelty she says she often witnessed, both to animals and people.)

By any standards, Ali was extremely successful and dedicated to his work. But he, too, felt the restrictions of living in Saddam's Iraq and was concerned about the nature of the society he was allowing his children to be brought into. He and Pauline resolved, in the mid-eighties, to relocate to England and make a new start for their young and growing family. To Pauline's enduring regret, their only opportunity to leave came and went in 1985, when Ali's elderly mother, who lived with them, suspected that Ali did not intend to return to Mosul from Lancashire after Jamal's birth. The ensuing hysterics, which played on the profound sense of duty he felt for his mother's care, were just too much. Ali promised his mother that he would return. A month after leaving, and having witnessed Jamal's birth, Ali came back to Mosul, to be followed, with resignation, not long after, by Pauline, Noor and the newborn.

While Pauline and Ali had decided to leave the misery of Mosul behind and start again in England – only to be thwarted by the matriarch – Margaret says she felt no pressure to leave Iraq. Olive had rejoined her after spending some time back in the United Kingdom following Thamir's death. She thought that being involved in bringing up her grandchildren in a hot and dry climate would be better for her long-term health than slow and stifling retirement in damp old Blighty. She helped Margaret make the new house a home, sewing curtains and cushion covers and, when the rest of the family went to Zuhair's mother's home each Friday for the regular family get-together, took on pet tasks like scouring the stove with vinegar until the brass burners shone like gold. Perhaps because she had already lived through the blitzes of World War II, Olive was much more vulnerable to the stresses of the constant wars visited on Iraq over her decades in Mosul. The howling of air-raid sirens, long nights spent with the children in bomb shelters during Operation Desert Storm, the food shortages, the funerals, the fear – eventually it all took its toll, and in the mid-nineties Olive took to her bed, where she has been ever since.

Domesticity was a refuge from the reality of war and Margaret's memories are of happy family times. "There was plenty of food around, we had lots of friends, and there were barbecues, holidays. We'd go off to the dam near Dohuk, where Germans had built workers' huts but which had been converted for tourists. Sometimes we would book the houses and get together to go for a couple of days. The kids could go down by the water. Other times, we'd go to Baghdad and stay at the Rashid Hotel. We'd take our swimsuits in those days – you could put your swimsuit on and go swimming in the pool. In the nineties, that changed and we'd just stay by the side of the pool and watch the boys. There was a Syrian restaurant called the Rota, where the food was beautiful. In Mosul there was the University Club, where we had New Year's parties, which were very good, and foreign films every week – they'd show them outside during the warm weather. Even in the university, sometimes, we had special events: the British Council used to bring Shakespeare troupes out, and we met the ambassador once. There was always something going on, though in later years it was just the men; when it started to go religious the women weren't really invited, except if there was a function for a visitor who was a woman, or a man who brought his wife. It really depended on the university president and which way the political wind was blowing."

6

"Not again ... "

" We had a couple of years of peace," Pauline said, sighing as she recalled the lull between wars. She and her family had just moved into the new house they'd built in the al-Hadba district of Mosul – named after the seventh-century leaning mosque tower on the other side of the Tigris – in July, 1989. The war with Iran had ended a year earlier, in a stalemate. Iraq had run out of money fighting the Iranians, and so could not afford to repair the damage inflicted on its oil infrastructure. The country's only real source of revenue was bust, the Ba'athist state was bankrupt and Saddam was thinking fast.

"We'd been in our house for just a month and were outside one day, fixing something, a fan, I think. I could hear a television on in someone else's house. Suddenly, I heard this voice screaming, the same voice that had screamed about the battles, the great victories won in the war with Iran. I said to Ali: 'Listen, he's screaming again.'

"So we went inside and put the television on, and the man on the television was screaming about how they'd invaded Kuwait. I was so depressed. All I could say was: 'Not again.'"

For a week or so leading up to the August, 1990, invasion, Saddam had been massing troops on the south-eastern border, threatening to march in and punish Kuwait for a range of apparent sins, including theft of Iraqi oil. He wanted to wipe out his massive debt to Kuwait, and he desperately needed a cause to focus the minds of an increasingly disillusioned populace. He knew invading Kuwait wouldn't be unpopular at home as many Iraqis believed their tiny neighbour was really part of their country anyway, stolen away when the great powers divvied up the globe after World War II. Nobody, least of all Saddam, believed there would be any resistance – indeed, it took the Iraqi army seven hours to overrun the entire country. But nor was there any widespread concern about the consequences of such aggression. As the Iraqi army crossed into Kuwait, scavengers followed in its tracks and proceeded to, literally, strip the country bare, like vultures swooping on a carcass and picking it clean. Across Iraq, there was a stunning consumer bonanza as the property of Kuwaitis, who lived in comparative luxury paid for with their petrodollars, was shifted, wholesale, north of the border. As Kuwait was systematically raided, the shops and markets of Iraq brimmed with products that hadn't been seen for years, if ever.

"What a way to raid a country," Iraqi artist Nuha al-Radi wrote in her book *Baghdad Diaries 1991–2002*. "Apparently we denuded Kuwait of everything plus the kitchen sink. Aeroplanes, buses, traffic lights, appliances, everything. Shops all over the country are full of their consumer goods. Imagine!"

Pauline said: "Everything you can imagine came in. McVitie's digestive biscuits, plates, washing liquids, Comfort for the washing machine, beautiful stuff from England and America that we'd never seen before. Different kinds of rice, Quaker oats, Lurpak butter. There were televisions, washing machines and air-conditioners, electric things that were still in their boxes. I didn't see many clothes. In Mosul getting things other than clothes was more important, especially the foodstuffs and electrical products for the home. People went crazy for the cars, the Cadillacs and other big American cars that came in. There was a hell of a lot of stuff, and people knew it was coming in from Kuwait."

Ali bought an air-conditioner from a patient who turned up at his clinic late one evening with eight used units on the back of a truck. "They were eight hundred dinars each. Ali told the man that he'd just finished building the house and didn't have much money. So he just took the one," Pauline said. Some people denied (and still do) that the massive looting of Kuwait was the source of their summer comfort, a telltale sign they knew they were doing wrong. Pauline said she initially thought her new air-conditioner had come, legitimately, from Basra, the southern port city that a lot of imported products are shipped through. "Ali said to me: 'What country do you think you're living in?' He justified it by saying that he had paid for it with his own money.

"I wasn't pleased, I didn't like it," she continued. "A relative gave Noor a toy organ, an instrument that you blow into that has musical keys. He was with security in Kuwait. The toy was from a child's bedroom. I never let her have it. I put it, still in its box, in a cupboard, and every time I looked at it, I thought of the poor child whose it had been, and wondered what had happened to that family."

Saddam Hussein's decision to send his army into Kuwait was, arguably, the first step on a long road leading, thirteen years later in March, 2003, to Operation Iraqi Freedom. President George Bush, the father, declared of Iraq's invasion of Kuwait: "This will not stand." He pulled together a broad, international coalition and won the backing of the United Nations to send troops in to force Saddam out. On January 17, 1991, Operation Desert Shield, in which hundreds of thousands of US troops had massed in Saudi Arabia, morphed into Operation Desert Storm, and the bombing of Iraq began.

But even as the drums of war began beating louder, it seems that few people in Iraq really believed that international opprobrium would take the form of a collective military punishment. Few bothered to stock up on essential food or water; everyone took a "wait and see" attitude, including Pauline and Ali, and Margaret and Zuhair. Perhaps the fabulous shopping frenzy they'd just experienced had lulled Iraqis into a comfortable zone of false normality.

The bombing was fearsome, Pauline remembers. "The weapons are much more sophisticated now, they're more accurate. But then it was all over the place. There were missiles flying all over the place that first day. You could see them flying over willy-nilly. We were trying to leave, and Ali was trying to get the car out but every time he got it halfway out, a missile would fly over and he'd have to go back into the garage." The bombers, she recalled, were "big and heavy and the house would shake and vibrate when the planes came over." After a few hours of what would have been a side-splitting, Keystone Kops-style cat-and-mouse sketch if it hadn't been so life-and-death terrifying, Ali eventually got the car out of the garage, and the family went to Gerver, where they stayed in the basement of a first cousin's house for two and a half weeks. "They'd built a new house with a toilet and running water. I enjoyed it because they make you feel like a queen; they cooked, washed the clothes, and the kids," Pauline said of the wartime break that is probably the only holiday she has ever had. When they came back to Mosul at the end of January, "it wasn't too bad. They'd driven him out of Kuwait by then," she says.

Iraq was facing tough times even before the Kuwait folly. From having been one of the most advanced countries in the Middle East, Iraq had sunk behind a religious veil as Saddam, publicly at least, swapped a rifle for a prayer mat as the prop in his ubiquitous propaganda posters, and was often shown on television and in newspapers praying or attending mosque. Saddam promoted a national piety as the salve for the chasm of poverty into which Iraq had been plunged by his misguided policies. Friday sermons became the vehicle for passing political directives to the masses.

"What the mullahs said on Fridays would let us know what the political tide was, they'd provide the guide to politically correct behaviour and thought," Pauline explained. The trend towards religion had become noticeable after the Iran–Iraq War as Saddam co-opted the faith in an effort to maintain control over potentially troublesome religious parties, especially the Shiite groups that identified with and were often supported by the Iranian theocracy. More women began to wear headscarves, and more men would tut in the street at women they thought inappropriately dressed. "It could be short sleeves, or trousers, wearing a lot of make-up, not wearing a headscarf. They'd tut to make you feel uncomfortable, but they'd take a nip at your bottom if they felt like it," said Pauline, tutting herself at the hypocrisy. "And they don't like red," she recalled. "I like red, but that was out. You could get away with something that had red in it, but no red shoes. It took a lot of getting used to." When I reminded her that Margaret, when I met her in Pauline's home a couple of days after Mosul's fall, had been wearing trousers, she said: "Because everything had collapsed, we felt as if we were free. So Margaret put trousers on."

The Friday sermons were blared through loudspeakers so no one in the neighbourhood had an excuse for not knowing the current line, and the topics ranged from the geopolitical to the mundane. When United Nations weapons inspectors were on their way in, the mullahs would proclaim the country free of weapons of mass destruction. When doctors (a particular hatred of Saddam's dating back to 1959, when he was shot while taking part in an abortive attempt to assassinate Brigadier Abdul Karim Ali, the head of state, and hadn't been able to find a doctor to treat him) raised their fees, the mullahs railed against them. When, during the rationing of the nineties, housewives had to take their flour to bakeries to be made into bread and suspected the bakers were selling the good-quality flour on the black market, the mullahs singled out the bakers for criticism. In their sermons, they banged on about Palestine, about the West, about America, Christians, Kurds, about the rubbish shown on television – a dig at illegal satellite dishes, rather than the interminable local programming on Saddam.

"One day, Ali came back from mosque and was really angry. He said he'd stood there feeling like he was being personally insulted – the mullah had gone on about how bad Kurds are, how bad doctors are, how bad foreigners are. And there's him, a Kurdish doctor with a foreign wife," Pauline said. "Another time, the mullah had been having a go at the Christians, and at the end of the sermon, as people were leaving, there was a big Christian guy standing outside the mosque with a pipe in his hand. He went in and hit the mullah with the pipe."

As religious fervour took hold, Pauline began to wonder at the changes in the people around her. Suddenly, men she'd known for years were pulling away when she went to shake hands with them, now finding it "haram," or forbidden, to touch a woman who was not their wife or immediate family. "I said to Ali, I don't know where I am any more."

By mobilizing the army once more, in late 1990, Saddam gave his battle-hardened troops something to do for a few months. But once they were driven out of Kuwait, things only got worse. The United States and the United Nations may not have had a mandate to remove Saddam from power in 1991, but they imposed crippling conditions that were, in part, aimed at pushing straitened Iraqis into rising up against the man to blame for their plight. Those who did, however – Shiites (adherents of an Islamic sect who form a minority within the religion as a whole but who make up the majority of the population in Iraq and Iran) and Kurds who believed they had Washington's backing – were cruelly suppressed. Saddam, the arch manipulator, made sure Iraqis, and many in the international community, believed he and his country were the victims of American perfidy rather than of his own disastrous ineptitude, corruption and vanity.

"After 1991, life started to deteriorate, because of the sanctions. Previous to that, we had a fantastic life," Margaret said. "We'd go to the club every Thursday night; we'd go until one or two o'clock in the morning. In the spring, every Friday, we'd go on a picnic or a barbecue by the river. But from 1991, people couldn't afford to live as they had. There wasn't anything coming into the country. People started to live on government rations. Inflation was high, wages were low. Before the war, it was all subsidized by the government. That's why the wages were enough, because the government had money. Whatever had been available in the markets fell by about fifty per cent and what we got was rubbish from Indonesia, Malaysia, Jordan – it all came in as rations."

The sanctions initially froze all Iraqi assets overseas and banned all imports and exports, except medical supplies and, in the case of "humanitarian circumstances," food. This was meant to ensure that Saddam did not rebuild the military or pursue his well-known ambition to amass an arsenal of weapons of mass destruction. As a result, anything that could possibly have been used, in any way imaginable, as a component in a hardware or software application that could be put to military use was banned from entering Iraq. From computer chips, to nuclear medicine, to lead pencils. Young Iraqis graduated from university with degrees in advanced computer technology equipped with knowledge the West had left behind in the eighties, Margaret's older twin, Ali, among them. People died of what should have been easily remedied medical complaints. Child malnutrition levels, as well as premature births, and deaths of women in labour, rose alarmingly. "When my mother was in hospital, she needed radiotherapy treatment, but she couldn't have it because of the isotopes," Zuhair told me that day in early 2006 when I met him in London, when he'd curled his stockinged feet underneath him and slowly smoked. Isotopes are a component of nuclear medicine, widely used to treat cancer; they are also present in nuclear weapons. "There were many thousands of people with cancer, children with leukaemia, who couldn't get treatment, who died. And now there are raised radiation levels because of the depleted uranium used in American weaponry. If we protest, they will say it is because they brought freedom and democracy. But we are not free and we do not have democracy. But now we have radiation, and the diseases it causes."

Eventually, in the mid-nineties, the United Nations allowed Iraq to export oil in return for humanitarian assistance – the so-called oil-for-food programme. Saddam used oil-for-food concessions to buy and reward loyalty. "People who didn't have two pennies to rub together before are now multimillionaires from smuggling," Zuhair went on. "And still the people suffer. When corruption comes, it spreads like a virus. When you bring in one corrupt person, soon everyone will be corrupted, or they will be excluded. Plenty of people were benefiting from the sanctions system, including Iraqis, both in the government and with connections to government."

But mostly, as he said, Iraqi people suffered terribly. Hyperinflation forced people on to the streets because wages were no longer enough to buy food. By the mid-nineties, according to the scholars Peter Sluglett and his late wife Marion Farouk-Sluglett, a middle-ranking civil servant's monthly income was 5,000 dinars, but a chicken cost 4,000 dinars. Many who could leave the country did so, and by 1996, they say, around 3 million people, what they estimate to be 15 per cent of the population, had moved abroad. The cabal around Saddam accumulated vast fortunes by exploiting the rationing system, speculating on foreign currency movements and illegally trading oil. Before sanctions, one dinar was worth $3.10; by the end of the decade, $1 was worth 3,000 dinars. The Englishwomen managed to stay above water: Ali's many commitments brought in enough to keep the family clothed and fed; Olive's British pension, and rent from a tract of land that Zuhair had inherited from his father, helped to top up what Margaret and Zuhair had coming in. But as a ranking party member and senior bureaucrat, far from being the recipient of government largesse in handing out staples, Zuhair was often asked to contribute to the purchase of sheep that would be slaughtered and distributed to the poor.

For many Iraqis, destitution loomed, and Pauline noticed that the number of people appearing on the street to sell their own possessions – everything from shoes to furniture and, when things were truly desperate, their wedding gold, always the last to go – mushroomed, as did the numbers knocking on her door each day asking for food and money.

"In Islam, if someone comes to your home and asks for help, it's a very bad mark against you if you don't give them something. It's give and take. After Desert Storm the begging became awful. Everything was terribly expensive and would get even more expensive in July when the crops came in because the farmers were subsidized by the government. The currency was revalued, with a couple of zeros added to the notes, which meant the dinar was worth very little but the salaries stayed the same. So more people became beggars.

"People used to send their children to ask if they could sweep. People would knock on the door, asking for alms. If it was kids, then that's an industry, they'd be driven to the estate in a bus, and it was the same kids every day. I wouldn't even answer the door. But often it was an old lady, or an old man, and I'd give them money or a bag of meat from the freezer."

With a good income from his positions at the hospital and the university, and his clinic, Ali was able to buy meat every week. "But the majority could not afford meat, and used to have to buy the cheaper cuts of not-so-good meat or the local fish. A lot of people just used to have rice and soup, and the soup would have vegetables in it, sometimes beans or chickpeas, which are good sources of protein," Pauline remembered. Knowing themselves to be comparatively well off, they gave their rations to relatives who lived near by and had nine children, and who were so stretched they did without meat for years.

The appearance of children and the elderly begging for work and food was just one consequence of the sanctions. The quality of the supplies people received was so poor, Pauline said her children had terrible stomach cramps from the bread, which was often grey; Margaret said that milk powder, especially important for young children, was sometimes unavailable for months on end. People took to growing vegetables and raising chickens or sheep in their gardens. Malnourished children couldn't concentrate at school, many of which didn't have paper or pencils, let alone textbooks and other teaching materials. Intellectual activity stagnated as Iraqi scholars and professionals no longer had access to literature from abroad that would help them keep up with developments in their fields. Older people sickened and died, as Zuhair's mother had, from lack of medicines that were, theoretically, available and affordable. Professionals, such as teachers, could no longer make ends meet and had to take on what extra work they could to earn money to feed their families. People's homes fell apart around them because there was nothing available for upkeep and repairs. The same was true of industry – factories, power stations, telecommunications, roads, sewerage and water purifying plants, hospitals, everything was eventually run into the ground and all but ceased to function. Government offices, hospitals and some hotels and businesses had generators they could fall back on during the frequent power cuts. Ordinary people couldn't afford the fuel. Animal vaccines were not permitted, so livestock died. Fertilizers and insecticides were banned, so crop yields diminished. Iraq and Iraqis were cut off from the rest of the world. And while Saddam Hussein refused to bow to international pressure and comply with conditions that would have seen the sanctions lifted, he shifted the blame to the West, the United Nations and Britain, France and the United States.

The constant scrabbling for food that became part of life under the oil-for-food rationing regime was dreary and degrading. The rations served the purpose only of bare sustenance; there was no joy in eating as housewives like Margaret and Pauline were forced to do the best they could with food they wouldn't have served to cattle before the country began to starve. Margaret went from making choux pastry to sifting the chaff from her monthly ration of flour. "The flour was disgusting," she remembered with a shudder. "It had weevils in it, you'd have to sieve it and you'd see them jumping about. And it was full of bran. [Pauline recalled people collecting the bran from their flour rations and selling it as horse fodder.] You couldn't find the white flour. Flour, washing powder, soap and these things went off the market. Milk was all powdered and there wasn't always enough to go around."

Food shortages in the city had become so severe in the years immediately after Desert Storm that many people returned to their villages, to the land, so they could eat. Of the people who stayed in the cities, it was pretty much only those who traded for a living who did well; most others barely got by on the government handouts. After 1996, rations were doubled. Each person received 20 pounds of flour, 7 pounds of rice, 2¾ pounds of cooking oil, 1 pound of lentils, half a pound of beans, 1 pound of powdered milk, 4½ pounds of sugar, one third of a pound of tea, half a pound of soap, and three-quarters of a pound of detergent. For this, they would have to line up at a designated agent, usually a neighbourhood shop, and have it weighed out for them. If there was no tea, for instance, or milk or soap when they got there, they just went without and hoped it would come in the following month. The monthly rations for Margaret's family of eight cost them a total of US$1.50; the government paid the rest, which at $5 a head came to $38.50. In this way, Saddam's regime was praiseworthy for subsidizing the meagre rations that the heartless international community permitted his people. Meanwhile, much of what arrived in the country, certainly the good-quality produce, was re-exported by government cronies for hard currency. While the world saw television footage of Iraqi babies dying for lack of milk, milk powder that had been earmarked for Iraq showed up in the markets of neighbouring countries such as Syria and Jordan.

Margaret refused to raise chickens, she said, because she didn't want the accompanying filth and the likelihood that they would attract rats. But the cost of eggs rose so high that chickens and eggs became currency.

Nuha al-Radi tells in her *Baghdad Diaries* of an acquaintance who was letting a room in his house for two trays of eggs a month. "Now the tenant is losing money as the price of eggs rises ever upwards," she wrote. She also reported how nauseatingly desperate the situation became for some, when "parents are beating up their children because they can then be hospitalised for up to three weeks – there they can be fed." Anything that people wanted or needed above the rations they had to buy on the open market, and as the chickens and eggs illustrate, prices were exorbitant, out of reach of most people. And because so many people had returned to the land, vegetable and fruit supplies to the cities often ran short, too. "There was always something that wasn't available and you just had to learn to do without," Margaret said. Added Pauline: "If you had the money you could find anything. I feel very lucky and blessed because many decent people went without many things and struggled to feed and dress their families. These are the real heroes."

Hard times became even harder, and xenophobia became part of the Iraqi political landscape and national identity as the Ba'ath focused on its enemies as the cause of all the country's ills to deflect attention from its own self-serving ways. A good patriot was defined by the depth of his hatred for Washington, London and the West. Racism escalated, and both Pauline and Margaret found themselves deflecting abuse that ranged from a sarcastic "How are you?" in the street to graffiti scrawled on walls, youths standing outside the house screaming insults, schoolyard attacks on their children. Margaret's three tall, strapping, fair-skinned lads had each other as back-up, and a teacher of Alia's made a point one day of telling the class that her mother had Arab blood. "Helping out," Margaret called the lie that made her daughter acceptable. Noor was once knocked flying across a room by a girl twice her size who had taken a dislike to her. "My kids did have a hard time because they were half English," Pauline said, "but they never said they didn't want to go to school, they had to grow up and look after themselves."

She might brush it off now, but the legacy of a decade or more of racial bridge-playing has left a shadow of weariness over Pauline, though there is no residue of resentment because in her own home, and among her family, she was thoroughly accepted. She lived in a house of four languages – Arabic, Kurdish, Gerver and English – and so she remained shy of natural fluency in Arabic, which may have been a contributing factor among those with a propensity for bigotry. Margaret did well with the language, having only one to learn, but unlike Pauline, who can pass, at a glance, as Arab, that is not the case for her. Tall, slim and blonde, there is no mistaking Margaret as anything but a European. So each woman, in her way, had to deal with the fall-out of Saddam's deft deflection of disquiet away from his government and towards the innocents within.

"I've been an Iraqi longer than you," Margaret used to say to any younger person cheeky enough to ask her where she was from. Like all foreign residents, she'd been forced to give up her passport and officially change her nationality to Iraqi. "There's no Iraqi as tall as you, you can't be Iraqi," they'd say, and she'd have to hold down a rage that boiled up when her place in the country was attacked.

The daily grind and the political oppression were compounded by the fear of missile attacks by Allied warplanes that many people in Iraq believed were deliberately drawn to civilian targets. The warplanes patrolled "no-fly zones" that were established in the north, at the 36th Parallel, and so included Mosul, and also over the south, first at the 32nd and then the 33rd Parallel just south of Baghdad, to prevent Saddam setting his military against the northern Kurds and the southern Shiites, who had separately tried to rebel against the Ba'ath government only to be murderously – genocidally, some say – suppressed. American, British and French military jets regularly patrolled these zones and Iraqi anti-aircraft guns would regularly appear on suburban streets, awaiting orders to fire on the Allied craft. If the weapons locked on to an Allied aircraft, they would often be detected and then automatically fired upon. Such attacks could wipe out entire residential blocks, or factories, or military installations, or hospitals, or schools. Locals, including Pauline and Ali, have told me they believe this was a deliberate strategy of Saddam's, "so he could point at the civilian deaths," Pauline said, "and say to the world, 'look what they are doing to us.'" An acquaintance of Pauline's who manned an anti-aircraft gun had been killed this way. On the day that one of the enormous batteries appeared on the corner of her street, she said, "there was sheer panic until it disappeared again."

The northern no-fly zone, through which Iraqi planes could not fly, and the line of control, across which Iraqi soldiers could not move, resulted in the delineation of an autonomous "Kurdistan." Kurds who had fled Saddam's attacks now felt safe enough to return to their homes. Many had entered Iran, but the Turkish government, which has long suppressed its own large population of Kurds, would not allow Iraqi Kurds to enter, and in the freezing winter conditions many thousands died of exposure and disease in the mountains along the border. The suppression of the 1991 Kurdish revolt saw the United States come to the rescue with Operation Provide Comfort, bringing in relief supplies and chaperoning survivors back to their homes. International aid organizations brought in donated food and clothing. This had a knock-on benefit for the people struggling to makes ends meet in the median strip between the two patrolled regions, as a lot of the clothing and textile products that came into Iraqi Kurdistan would soon be found in the cities on the other side of the line of control. Suddenly, markets sprang up selling clothing, blankets, leather jackets, shoes, tablecloths, towels, all of it still in the wrapping as it was probably excess export production from Turkish textile factories. And because it was classified as second hand, it was cheap. "These things being available made it possible for people to survive," said Pauline, who went regularly with Noor to a huge basement market in central Mosul. Drivers who were risking their lives, as Iraqi soldiers patrolling the internal border often shot at cars and even villagers, brought the goods across the line of control. It is quite likely that the authorities allowed the markets to flourish because they were the only outlets that sold clothing most people could afford. Manufacturers habitually produce 5–10 per cent over contracted quantity, in case they need to make up for faults, and this excess often makes it on to street stalls at knocked-down prices. In Iraq, these back-door goods ended up in markets like that in downtown Mosul, or on carts that men would push through residential streets. "Where it might cost twenty-five thousand dinars for a pair of trousers for a child, at the market you could buy trousers and shoes and a couple of shirts and jumpers and a coat for that. They were fantastic. You could tell they were meant for overseas, as there were T-shirts with Thomas the Tank Engine on, or football strips from Liverpool or Everton. A lot of the stuff had labels on for Marks & Spencer, or Littlewoods, or BHS. There were Adidas and Nike tracksuits," said Pauline. "It became a big business for some people who got rich doing it. But it was a godsend for people who were getting poorer all the time."

As the people became poorer, so their morale plummeted, and their frustrations were turned on each other. By 2003, two generations of Iraqis had known only the oppression and violence that were the monopoly of Saddam's state; a generation had grown up knowing only war. There were no toys, so children played with rifles they fashioned from lengths of wood and used to pretend to shoot each other in the streets. Schoolyards became arenas where teachers were injured when they tried to break up fights. Domestic violence became a serious problem. Children mimicked adults, often giving outlet to their own latent brutality in cruelty towards pet animals or the puppies of wild dogs, or squirrels that were caught and tied up and poked with sticks. This is the behaviour of people lacking self-respect, and it is not unusual in countries where there are no individual freedoms or rights. The example comes from the top, from leaders who exhort their people to hate, who force schools to teach children to hate. Saddam Hussein seemed to think it was a devilishly clever joke to tile the foyer of the Al-Rashid Hotel in Baghdad with a huge mural of the first American President Bush, so that all who entered would have to walk over his face. Iraqis consider it insulting to be shown or hit with the bottom of a shoe, and it became a familiar image after the Ba'ath government fell, in 2003, to see Iraqis using their sandals to batter posters, murals and statues of Saddam.

Pauline said that American and British flags would be drawn in coloured chalk on the footpaths of Mosul's downtown streets, and government agents would hide close by to make sure the flags were dutifully trampled underfoot by pedestrians. "After Desert Storm, if something was going on like the UN weapons inspectors coming in to search for nuclear weapons, they'd try to whip things up and you'd see the flags on the street," she said. "I didn't like it, but I didn't want to draw attention to myself. If anyone had asked me anything, I would have said the right thing with my fingers crossed behind my back. I was afraid of being stopped in the street, as a lot of people were, and asked what I thought of America or Britain, so we used to avoid going anywhere to get into a conversation about it." And while at home, she lived in fear of someone painting an anti-American or anti-British slogan on her wall, as her first instinct, she said, would have been to go straight out and wash it off, no matter what it said.

And so life lurched on: Saddam defiant, the people suffering, children dying. A gravedigger in Baghdad told the Norwegian journalist Asne Seierstad, in early 2003, that he buried up to thirty children every day. Occasionally, throughout the nineties, international media would report on what was happening in Iraq, but, generally, its misery slipped into the miasma of long-running sagas.

Most of the foreigners who had come with their Iraqi spouses, and who had not left during the Iran–Iraq War, or the invasion of Kuwait, or Desert Storm, left now. Pauline and Margaret remembered that some friends who had escaped during the eighties had begun to dribble back, at least on exploratory visits, after 1988. But they soon read the runes and left again. Now, as the country sank to sub-Saharan levels of poverty and developmental disintegration, "gradually everyone disappeared, went when they could. So it was just me and Margaret, and one or two others," Pauline said, sighing.

The two Englishwomen of Mosul got on with raising their families. Margaret and Zuhair were able to send their four children to what were considered good schools, first a twenty-minute drive away and then, when a new school opened up on their housing estate, they could walk. There, they fared a little better than children at most schools, where texts had to be photocopied or shared, and pencils used down to the last, tiny nub. The teachers were strict, so Alia passed through to architecture at Mosul University – though what her degree earned her in applicable knowledge would have been comparable to Ali's computer degree, and Omar's veterinary science qualifications, a decade or more behind the rest of the world. Taleb, whose name means "student" in Arabic, ironically had no interest in book learning, much to his father's disappointment and his mother's annoyance. He did scrape into university, though not before he had been held back to repeat his third year of secondary school because his grades were too low to even take the end-of-year exam. He finally made it to a science degree he never had any intention of completing. In that respect, at least, circumstances were in his favour.

Pauline said Ali had no insight into the comparative merits of different schools and, considering that the state-set syllabus was the same across the country, thought they were much of a muchness. "The schools aren't good, the standards aren't high, there isn't any real teaching," Pauline said. "I didn't know anyone to give me advice. My friends had left, so I had no contact with anyone who knew about the schools. Ali didn't know, either, because he had gone to school in the village. The syllabus was all the same, and the learning was by rote, memorizing. In Iraq, if you have the ability to learn things parrot fashion, you're OK. There is no analysis or lateral thought involved, just how to learn it by heart, so when the question came up on an exam the students could answer it word for word as it appeared in the text."

There were some highlights to break up the hardship. Alia fell in love with a fellow student, a young man from Jordan, and the family travelled to Amman in 2002 for their wedding. The photographs of the day show

Alia radiantly happy in a beautiful white, sleeveless wedding gown, with flowers in her hair. Men and women are dancing together, and she and her bridegroom are a picture of joy as they are carried aloft to the reception. Well, the tutting over the pictures when Margaret showed them to her friends and relatives in Mosul could be heard back in Amman. "I didn't dare show the one of her being lifted up by the men," Margaret said, looking mortified at the thought of the reaction. Moslawis prefer their brides sullen; only the men dance at weddings, while the women remain seated, chatting as they watch their menfolk having all the fun.

For Pauline, the low point of this slow-playing misery came in 2001, when her mother called to say that her sister, Mary, younger by more than ten years, was dying of cancer. She'd found it impossible to maintain regular contact since the Iran–Iraq War. Before then she'd been able to telephone once a week. Then nothing for eight years. And, latterly, only intermittently. She immediately made her way to Jordan, and then to Britain, where she nursed her sister through the final months of her life.

7

A Horseman on the Horizon

On September 11, 2001, terrorists flew passenger jets into the World Trade Center in New York, and the Pentagon in Washington, killing thousands.

In Iraq, people danced in the streets. When asked why, they said Americans had got what they deserved.

That was the official line. In reality, people were nervous. They seriously believed their government could have been behind one of the worst atrocities in modern history.

"When we saw 9-11 on the television, we thought, oh no, they're going to think we did it," Pauline said. "We thought it would give America an excuse to turn on Saddam. And people did think, honestly, that Saddam might have had some role to play."

As the build-up to Operation Iraqi Freedom grew like a dust cloud on the horizon, people began stocking up on food and water. They crossed the line of control, risking Iraqi army sniper fire on their way into Kurdistan and, when they returned, arrest and imprisonment, to buy contraband satellite dishes. Once the war came, as everyone knew it would, they didn't want to miss a shot. Soon, for the first time since the Iran–Iraq War, when Saddam had banned them so that only the good news got through, satellite dishes were being openly sold in Mosul. They were selling out as fast as the shops could restock.

"We weren't frightened of the secret police any more," Pauline says. "Everyone knew change was coming."

8

Diary of a War

OPERATION FREE IRAQ

48 hours to go …

It feels like a sentence has been passed. People are busy saving water, buying food and joining lines for petrol. People are angry and I don't blame them. We just sit and wait.

24 hours to go …

The tension is immense; you can cut it with a knife. The streets are deserted. My husband has just been given a beautiful computer and all he can think about is – will it arrive on time?

Everyone is clearing their shops, offices and clinics, taking all their equipment to their homes. We eat our evening meal and I telephone my friend who I love very much; we wish each other God's protection. Here we watch the TV and sleep, but aware all the time that these are the last few hours of peace.

Operation Iraqi Freedom, as the Allied attack on the country is dubbed, begins just after dawn on March 20, 2003, with the bombing of a house in Baghdad where, the Americans say, President Saddam Hussein and one of, or maybe even both, his notoriously vicious sons are staying. The house, and much of the surrounding neighbourhood, is destroyed – but neither Saddam nor his boys Uday and Qusay are anywhere near it. This air strike is accompanied by a land invasion as thousands of troops cross the border from bases in Kuwait. The war has begun.

March 20 (Day 1)

This morning at 4 a.m. we were awake, my little dog wanted to go outside. Quickly I ran to the garden with her. It was about 6 a.m. that we heard from Syrian TV that the war had started. We hastily prepared mattresses under the stairs, the air raid sirens went off at about 9 or 9.30 a.m. but we heard and saw nothing in Mosul.

It is 5 p.m. now and it has been quiet. We will see what the night brings.

It's now 8 p.m. I've just turned on the radio to listen to the BBC. They have just told us that there are convoys on the move and heavy artillery fire.

Turkey has granted permission to the USA and Britain – this is not good for us in Mosul. [*This Pauline heard as rumour, which turned out to be unfounded; Turkey did not give the Allies permission to use its bases for launching attacks on Iraq and the original plan for a northern front, which had aimed to squeeze Saddam's forces in a north–south pincer, was thwarted. The bombing campaign was conducted from carrier groups parked in the Persian Gulf, coordinated on the ground by small units of American special forces, working with Kurdish peshmerga, who pinpointed targets and called in air strikes.*]

Another air raid siren at about 10.45 p.m. Still we haven't heard any planes, just the anti-aircraft guns. We don't think we will have much sleep.

March 21 (Day 2: Spring Day)

Spring Day marks the equinox and has for thousands of years been celebrated as the Zoroastrian New Year, known in Persian as Nouruz and by the Kurds (who live predominantly in Iraq, Iran, Syria and Turkey) in their own dialect as Newruz. Zoroastrianism is thought to be the original monotheistic religion; the birth of its prophet, Zoroaster, is put at around 1,000 BC and his ideological influence spread to China, India, Central Asia, Persia and the Middle East, and as close to Europe as Armenia and Turkey. Some scholars believe Zoroaster's teachings – equality of all, hard work and good deeds – helped shape the major religions of today: Christianity, Judaism, Islam and Hinduism. Small communities still exist around the world, notably India's Parsees, who are known for leaving their dead out for vultures in their own version of the endless cycle of ashes to ashes, dust to dust. Zoroastrians worshipped fire as the symbol of the creator's energy – and so fire is central to Nouruz/Newruz celebrations.

The 2003 spring equinox passes on March 21, and on this day fires burn on hilltops all over Iraqi Kurdistan, billowing thick, stinking, petrochemical smoke from the old tyres used to fuel the flames. Groups of peshmerga militiamen stand around these fierce orange bonfires, proud and poised, flickering sentinels silhouetted against the starry twilight.

Many people living in the cities of Kurdistan pack up their cars to return to their villages, as they do every year to celebrate Newruz with their clans. This happy exodus has been misinterpreted by a lot of foreign reporters and aid workers as pre-war fright and flight. The Red Crescent in neighbouring Iran has shipped in thousands of tents and supplies and built refugee camps in anticipation of a massive flood of terrified people over the Iraqi border. And they are sure that the holiday travellers who began their journeys a couple of weeks earlier were the advance trickle of this expected surge. But as soon as the New Year holiday is over, most people come happily home to the cities again.

Newruz 2003 is a time of anticipatory joy and thanksgiving for the Kurds of northern Iraq, who understand too well the reality of war, having endured it for millennia. They welcome the Allied invasion as a long-overdue, true liberation from the tyranny of Saddam. They believe that even if some stray armoury comes their way (as it does on a couple of occasions with fatally tragic results), it is an aberration, the unavoidable collateral fall-out of battle, a bump on the road to the freedom and power they can now taste as a bitter but welcome salve for centuries of injustice.

For Pauline, her family and neighbours, and the people of Mosul, Newruz 2003 is not a time for gaiety. On the wrong side of history and the wrong side of international demarcation, the "line of control" that protects Iraqi Kurdistan from Saddam's wrath, they can only hunker down, wait and pray, seeing themselves in the firing line of a battle between two implacable, immovable opponents.

I cry because guns and prayers don't mix.

4 a.m. Again the sirens and the guns are very heavy. We are tired and drowsy; we drift off to sleep.

At about 7.30 a.m. again the sirens and the guns.

8 a.m. Listening to the BBC for the news. The army has entered the south and Basra is under heavy bombardment and also Baghdad.

10.30 a.m. They say on the radio Royal Marines have taken Fao [*a small port by the Shatt al-Arab, near the Persian Gulf*].

Today is Spring Day, also Kurdish Day. I'm afraid there will be no dancing today.

1 p.m. News coming in reports heavy fighting in Kirkuk around the oilfields and the city. Reports of a helicopter crash in Kuwait, British and American troops are killed. May God bless them.

Prayers in the mosque took place all over Mosul. People are walking in the street, no air raids since this morning. We will see what the night will bring.

8 p.m. We heard from the TV that a vast attack has been launched on Baghdad. Five minutes later the air raid siren begins again and the guns go off.

I see things from the TV which I never thought I would see. Attacks on Mosul and Kirkuk last until 1.30 a.m. and the air raid sirens signal the end of the air raid. A man from a town near the border is hitting Saddam's picture with a slipper, a big insult in Iraqi culture.

March 22 (Day 3)

The Allied invasion is reaching its full strength as soldiers and materiel pour into Iraq from Kuwait, and the bombing of the cities escalates to what feels like a frenzied firestorm. In Britain, the first sign of what media freedom advocates are calling "patriotic censorship" appears when Sir Ray Tindle, head of a provincial media company called Tindle Newspapers which has more than 150 local titles, bans his editors from publishing stories critical of the Blair government's decision to join the United States in the war on Iraq. "So much for the right to know, free speech and all those other rights which our forefathers fought to establish," says the National Union of Journalists. It emerges in London that Margaret Wilmhurst, one of the senior legal advisers to Foreign Secretary Jack Straw, has resigned because she is unhappy with the government's insistence that the United Nations' resolutions on Iraq provided adequate and acceptable justification for waging this war. Mrs Wilmhurst does not want to be associated with a decision that she does not think is based in international law.

The night was quiet after 1.30 a.m. We sleep well and up until now things in Mosul are peaceful. We listen to the radio and learn 1,000 missiles have been launched over Iraq. They say Baghdad looks like hell. God be with the people.

1.30 a.m. Air raid sirens go again and last about 20 minutes. I'm looking at some horrific pictures on the television, just total destruction. A little girl with her head bandaged, crying. It just about says it all.

11.45 p.m. No sleep during the night. Many planes overhead and the guns are firing at them. The noise is unbearable.

March 23 (Day 4)

Millions of people across the world march to protest the war. From Barcelona to Brisbane, Montreal to Mogadishu, Cairo to Calcutta. More than 250,000 people protest in New York, and a couple of days later another few hundred hold a "die in" on Fifth Avenue in Manhattan – some are arrested for blocking the traffic. Buddhist monks beat drums in the South Korean capital of Seoul, schoolchildren stage classroom strikes in Britain, Germany and Thailand. In Bangladesh, Northern Ireland and Syria, tens of thousands of people take to the streets, voicing the same anti-war message as marchers in Iran, Colombia and Algeria. Throughout the first two weeks of the invasion and bombardment of Iraq, disgust with the war unites millions across every divide – national, ethnic, cultural, linguistic, religious. Young and old, poor and rich, aristocrat and labourer, intellectual and not so cerebral, men and women, left and right. There are those, of course, from each of these categories who support the invasion of Iraq, but they don't seem to have the numbers ...

00.30 a.m. One air raid is finished and five minutes later another one begins. Even worse than the first. Just like the First Gulf War the little dogs that run wild start to bark and alert us to the planes coming.

Another air raid at about 4.30 a.m. which lasts until about 8.30 a.m. We are so tired we just sleep through and hope.

10.30 a.m. We see the pictures of Baghdad and Tikrit. It's an utter disgrace to see such suffering and devastation.

Someone should drop a couple of these bombs on the children of Bush and Blair and see how they would like it.

11.45 a.m. Another air raid and I am still writing with the bombing overhead. Something nice – my Mama rings me from England. I am so glad to hear her voice. She tells me people are ringing her from all over, praying for us. We cry and I tell her we love her.

1 p.m. Air raid sirens tell us the air raid is over.

1.45 p.m. Air raid again, very heavy. God help us.

Nothing to report. News pretty much the same. It's going dark now. People have been outside, kids playing. See what the night brings.

The night brought hell from 8 p.m. until 8 a.m. this morning, just continuous bombing. Factories, palaces, all gone.

Plans for a northern assault against the Iraqi leadership are taking shape as tensions on the frontier that divides the free Kurdish area from the dictator's domain spill into sporadic shooting and air strikes are called in against the forces of Saddam.

US special forces are active around Irbil, the capital of Iraqi Kurdistan, supervising the rapid renovation of airstrips in the city and at Harir, in a nearby valley, which it is believed will be used to land Allied forces in readiness for the move south.

Four American landings were reported near the northern city of Sulaymaniyah yesterday, at the Bakrajo airstrip 16 kilometres away, disgorging scores of US military personnel.

American soldiers were also spotted shopping at a supermarket in Irbil, the capital of the Kurdish northern region.

Mr Giuseppe Renda, head of the Irbil delegation of the Red Cross, said 3,000 people had fled their homes close to what they expect will be the front lines.

Refugees who had fled Mosul and Kirkuk, which remain under Saddam's control, had been taken to the village of Diana, near the border with Iran, he said.

Massive flashes regularly lit up the night sky over the foothills of the Cudi mountains yesterday as British and American bombers dropped their deadly payload on targets south of the front line marked by the Kalak river.

In the major oil-producing cities of Mosul and Kirkuk, bombing raids that are part of the Allied patrols that have protected the north from the will of Saddam for twelve years have been stepped up.

Cooperation between the Americans and the guerrilla armies of the two main Kurdish groups that between them control the vast regions of Iraq's north has become evident as the snail-like pace of the northern campaign picks up momentum.

Soldiers of the Kurdistan Democratic Party based in Irbil, and who control the eastern sector of the north, said air strikes had been ordered on a well-fortified Iraqi position south-west of the city.

Tracer fire from anti-aircraft guns was visible as troops manning the Iraqi defensive posts fired impotently into the air as the bombers passed too high to be hit.

Some defections of Iraqi troops over the river have been reported.

A Kurdish peshmerga guerrilla said some soldiers attempting to defect had been shot in the back as they moved towards no man's land.

On the Kalak frontier, where riverside villages have been deserted by fearful residents, Iraqi soldiers kept up an intermittent barrage of cannon fire.

Guerrillas on the frontier said Iraqi defensive positions had been reinforced with troops of the Republican Guard who were being sent from the south, an indication that Saddam is preparing for an assault. As tension mounts while waiting for the Americans to begin their campaign, the Iraqis fire on anyone who dares venture onto open ground. (Irish Times, March 24, 2003)

March 24 (Day 5)

9 a.m. Still the air raid siren hasn't gone from last night to signal the all clear; that's 13 hours of bombing. We feel this is hell. It's quiet at the moment, we have moved into the hallway downstairs, we will sleep on the floor from now on. May God help us.

The night again brings heavy bombing, one big crash breaks the windows of one of my friend's house and at my other friend's house the doors are jammed. My house rattles and shakes.

March 25 (Day 6)

Three air raids, up until 1 p.m. My husband is on call at the hospital. I just want him home. More air raids but the weather is very bad, the wind is very strong.

Night falls and even the weather doesn't stop the bombardment and it continues through the night.

March 26 (Day 7)

7 a.m. Heavy bombing again, the guns are all over the place. My husband and son go for petrol. They see damaged buildings and many anti-aircraft guns all over the place. Life seems to go on. People are in the streets, walking, but it's very dangerous.

1 p.m. The air raid siren goes for the end. That's lasted for six hours.

News from the radio says a missile hit the market place in Baghdad killing 14 and injuring many. Britain and American say it's not theirs but we have seen houses in the last Gulf War reduced to rubble, so to me it's possibly true.

The night was quiet, just a few thuds of the anti-aircraft guns. We manage to get a bit of sleep.

March 27 (Day 8)

Today not much going on in the North. They say American troops were airlifted into Irbil, in Kurdistan, so we sit and wait. People are going about their own business.

The afternoon was quiet until about 8 p.m., which unleashed hell.

In my whole life I have not heard anything like it. You can hear the planes and then the almighty crack.

These two men – Bush and Blair – have a lot to answer for, and maybe not in this life, but when it's their time they will have to stand in front of someone who is Greater than both of them and be made to answer for their actions. We see day after day the terrible pictures on the television. Small children suffering and hurt men crying in the streets.

March 28 & 29 (Days 9 & 10)

The morning is quiet and then at 12.30 again hell is unleashed. Three to four bombs on a factory near us. The house shakes, my husband is working and I wish he was here but I don't want him to leave the hospital until it's over.

After 15 minutes again the planes come back. The garage gates are blown and we can see them blowing in and out.

Can't these people leave us alone? All they are doing is turning the people against them.

March 30 (Day 11)

The day was very peaceful with a few anti-aircraft guns going off.

When the night time came, many planes could be heard and anti-aircraft guns responding.

March 31 (Day 12)

This week's issue of the New Yorker *magazine asks WHO LIED TO WHOM? Why did the administration endorse a forgery about Iraq's nuclear programme? The journalist Seymour Hersh writes: "Last September 24th, as Congress prepared to vote on the resolution authorizing President George W. Bush to wage war in Iraq, a group of senior intelligence officials, including George Tenet, the Director of Central Intelligence, briefed the Senate Foreign Relations Committee on Iraq's weapons capability. It was an important presentation for the Bush Administration. Some Democrats were publicly questioning the President's claim that Iraq still possessed weapons of mass destruction which posed an immediate threat to the United States. Just the day before, former Vice President Al Gore had sharply criticized the Administration's advocacy of pre-emptive war, calling it a doctrine that would replace a 'world in which states consider themselves subject to law' with 'the notion that there is no law but the discretion of the President of the United States.'"*

Mr Hersh's article tells in devastating detail the story of fraudulent documents that were cited first by the British government and then by the Americans as evidence that Saddam Hussein had been trying to purchase "significant quantities" of uranium to fuel his long-held ambition to produce nuclear weapons. The documents – which themselves were not made public until much later – were proof that the Iraqi regime presented a clear and present danger to the world, and supported Mr Blair's claim that Iraqi missiles armed with chemical or biological weapons could be launched on British positions within 45 minutes. Mr Hersh talked to experts who told him these documents were amateurish cut-and-paste jobs; obvious fakes (though we do not learn by whom they have been faked) with no basis in fact. The implication of his reporting is that the war has been launched, not only on the basis of a fiction, but also of a conspiracy.

In his book Chain of Command, *published after the war, Mr Hersh goes into greater detail about the manipulation of the information in the forged documents by the "Iraq hawks" in the White House and the Pentagon, as well as dubious and unchecked information on Saddam's chemical, biological and nuclear weapons programmes provided by Iraqi dissidents who were being paid millions of dollars by US government agencies at the behest of Vice President Dick Cheney. He also fills in the blanks from interviews by American and British agents of former officials of the Saddam regime, who assured their interrogators that all such weapons had been destroyed – as the International Atomic Energy Agency had been saying repeatedly ahead of the invasion – on Saddam's direct order soon after the first Gulf War.*

Mr Hersh provides well-sourced evidence that the governments of President George W. Bush, in Washington, and Tony Blair, in London, had knowingly distorted information, and lied, to justify their desire to bring war down on Iraq. The war, he says, was already a sure thing by February, 2002.

From this morning, planes continuously flying over but no bombing, the noise is from the anti-aircraft guns.

Quiet night. We managed to get a good night's sleep.

We hear they have bombed Bashaka, a little town near Mosul, which is famous in the area for growing olives.

April 1 (Day 13)

A beautiful morning. It seems crazy: the pear blossom and orange buds are on the trees in my garden and I am hanging my washing outside and there is an air raid going on.

A quiet day, but we see the terrible pictures on the television and listen to the news and what turns out to be a nice spring day is destroyed when we see all the suffering.

A good night, had a good sleep.

"IT'S TERRIFYING – THERE'S JUST NO WAY WE CAN DEFEND OURSELVES."
Northern Iraq: Five young defectors from Saddam Hussein's conscript army said they had abandoned their posts on the northern front lines to flee to the peace and safety of the liberated north because they could no longer stand the terror inflicted by a fierce US bombing campaign.

The story told by the men yesterday, hours after they had crossed no-man's-land to give themselves up to Kurdish guerrillas, suggests that the Iraqi regular forces holding the north are crumbling under the pressure of the unrelenting air campaign that has intensified in recent days.

Their account of conditions on the front line, however, contradicts the official Kurdish version, presented by government and militia leaders alike, that the Iraqi enemy facing them from the south has been demoralised by an ongoing shortage of food, clothing and equipment.

The five men, aged between 18 and 22, said they had waved down a car near their front-line posts in Sadao early yesterday morning and asked the driver to take them across the river that divides Saddam's territory from the protected Kurdish zones.

"We came across by car," said one of the men, who did not give their names to protect their families. All said they were from southern Iraq.

"During the bombing, we could see the peshmerga over on this side, so we asked the driver to bring us over, and he did."

The men, who said they had been on the northern lines for 50 days, were driven to their decision to defect by the incessant bombing by US B-52 bombers, which in recent days have carpet-bombed the Iraqi front lines, in some places just 200 metres from the peshmerga posts.

"It's been going on for six days, but three days ago it just got more intense. It's terrifying. Whenever we heard the planes coming we hid ourselves in our shelters," said one.

"There is just no way we can defend ourselves against that sort of onslaught. I don't know how many of the Iraqi soldiers have been killed by the bombs, but I can say I saw one man dead," said another.

Since last Thursday, the Iraqis have been moving back towards Kirkuk, in a tactical move that appears to be in preparation for the defence of the city, the jewel of the northern plain.

In some of the outposts abandoned by Iraqi troops as they moved 15 km back from Qoshtapa, Kurdish militiamen found gas masks, explosives, mines and pictures of Saddam Hussein.

Mr Hoshyar Zebari, the international relations director of the Kurdish Democratic Party, said that Kirkuk and nearby Mosul had been infiltrated by Saddam Hussein's Fedayeen, a reputedly fearsome division of black-garbed fighters that was formed after the Gulf War and is believed to be doggedly loyal to the Iraqi leader.

The Fedayeen "have broken every law of war, placing themselves in schools, mosques, hospitals, churches," Mr Zebari said.

On Sunday, he said, a group of Fedayeen had set up armed cells inside a monastery in the village of Alqosh, "an example of how desperate they are, that they are now using civilian and religious sites for their activities."

Behind the Fedayeen were regular troops and, behind them, to ensure there was no retreat by the conscripts, were lines of soldiers of the Republican Guard, also known for their devotion to Saddam, he said.

The Ba'athist troops were now being rotated, with men from the north being sent to the south, and vice versa, in another move designed to minimise desertions, Mr Zebari said.

He said that Saddam's troop numbers, possibly including the newly formed suicide squads, were being reinforced by fighters from "Islamic fundamentalists and terrorist groups" outside the country, including Syrians, Jordanians, Palestinians and north Africans.

The five defectors said that their only information about the allied campaign in the south of the country came from soldiers who had been transferred.

Any communications equipment had been taken from them two weeks ago.

Nevertheless, they had adequate army rations, and enough blankets to keep them warm during the long, sleepless nights at their posts. Their black leather army boots, which sat in a jaunty pile behind the door of their room in the Kalak KDP headquarters, were well made and in good condition.

The five, all small and slim, looked younger than their years. They wore baggy khaki uniforms, with hand stitching where sleeves and legs had been shortened, and long underwear in grey or green, visible below their trousers.

Kurdish officials said they would be sheltered in northern Iraq until after the war, when they would be free to return to their homes.

Any information they provided would be handed over to the Americans, who are now in command of military operations in the north.

Officials reported 12 Iraqi defections yesterday, all from the same area as the five hitchhikers.

Most had walked across the lines under cover of darkness – and in danger of being shot in the back by their commanding officers – and approached shepherds for help in finding a haven outside Saddam's control.

Despite KDP assurances that they would be well looked after, the men appeared uncertain about their fate and refused to answer questions about the war or Saddam Hussein "because," said one, "we don't know our destiny." But they said their defection was not motivated by a hatred of the regime or by hopes that the coalition campaign to remove the government of Saddam Hussein would prevail.

"I don't hate the Americans. Why would I hate the Americans? I just hate the bombing, not the American people," said one of the young men as he sat on a grimy blanket on the floor of their room.

"I don't have any feelings for or against Saddam Hussein either. We just came here to preserve our own souls, to take refuge here. We're not soldiers by choice, we were doing our national service and we found ourselves on the front line," he said. (Irish Times, *April 1, 2003)*

April 2 (Day 14)

From about 8 o'clock this morning, the planes are flying above my house. We can actually see them as if they are teasing the anti-aircraft guns. We sit in the garden and watch as they leave a trail of white smoke making patterns in the sky. The all-clear siren goes off at 1 p.m.

We will have to see where they hit – when we watch television later in the day, it looks like the little village that grows olives again.

1.30 p.m. Another air raid. The noise is awful.

This goes on until 7 p.m. and still the all clear hasn't sounded. They bombed a village where there were soldiers, and the airport. I don't think there will be any sleep tonight.

We managed a little sleep, a lot of banging, and then we drift off.

April 3 (Day 15)

8.30 a.m. Woken by planes but no banging. Air-raid sirens go but we see and hear nothing.

We hear from the radio there is heavy fighting between the Kurds and people from Mosul on the outskirts of the city.

According to the radio, invading troops are making rapid progress on

Baghdad, as far as the airport. We have no proof of this, we must wait and see.

Nothing much. Seems quiet.

April 4 (Day 16)

About 4.30 a.m. Awoken by an almighty crack, sounded like a missile, the explosion was very close. This was followed by heavy bombardment and anti-aircraft guns.

It's about 10.30 a.m. now and another air raid in progress. They say on the radio the Kurds are on the outskirts of the city.

The afternoon has been peaceful in spite of an air raid in progress. People cannot imagine how we go to sleep at night wondering if we will wake in the morning.

April 5 (Day 17)

The New York Times *reports that Hummers are "Detroit's hottest seller." A Hummer is the suburban retail model of the enormous Humvee armoured military vehicle made by General Motors for US army use in desert warfare. Thousands of Humvees are now roaring across Iraq, transporting American troops, and embedded correspondents, towards Baghdad. Arnold Schwarzenegger has had a Humvee for years, and during his Hollywood heyday was often to be seen driving the half-tonne machine through the boulevards of Santa Monica as he took his kids for ice cream. But it is the war on Iraq which has proved a boon for the gargantuan "sports utility vehicle." It carries the prestige premium of patriotism.*

Hummers cost around $120,000 and, for fuel efficiency, they rate about as well as a Rolls-Royce Silver Cloud – not much more than 10 miles to the gallon (or 4.5 kilometres per litre) for the 2003 H2 model. (The 1998, BMW-designed Silver Cloud does 11 miles to the gallon, cost

£155,000 new, and, unlike the standard model Hummer, came with walnut panelling, a self-closing boot and a picnic table.)

The head of the "International Humvee Owners Group" sums up the new hooray-Humvee mood of America, telling the newspaper of the mighty macho mobile: "It's a symbol of what we all hold so dearly above all else, the fact we have the freedom of choice, the freedom of happiness, the freedom of adventure and discovery, and the ultimate freedom of expression. Those who deface a Hummer in words or deed deface the American flag and what it stands for."

The worst day so far. From 1.30 p.m. until 7 p.m. bombing with cruise missiles near my house. Today I thought that my time had come. I sat on the floor of my garage with my children and little dog and cried openly for the people of Iraq.

What we have done to deserve this I cannot imagine. We are very frightened and if I live through this I will sue somebody for this suffering we have had to endure. I just want my Hershey Bar – they say when you get a Hershey Bar the war is over.

8.30 p.m. We are just having a cup of tea and watching the television when three massive cracks rip over the house. We are all in shock. This is just too much.

We sleep at about 10.30 p.m. but we are very frightened. The night was not too bad but still you can feel the shock all around you.

April 6 (Day 18)

10.30 a.m. The air-raid siren goes from the previous day to say it's all clear. Five minutes later the air-raid siren goes off again and the planes and the banging are too much.

The radio has just reported that one of the planes has fired on their own people and the Kurds just outside Mosul (now they know how we feel).

They say they have killed a top VIP from the Kurdish Party.

18 KILLED AS US DROPS BOMB ON ITS KURDISH WAR ALLIES

Gwar, Iraq: A friendly fire incident, in which an American bomb was dropped on a convoy of vehicles in northern Iraq, claimed at least 18 lives yesterday, including a Kurdish translator working with BBC correspondent Mr John Simpson, who escaped with slight injuries.

A senior commander of the local Kurdish peshmerga forces, Mr Wajih Barzani, brother of Kurdish leader Mr Massoud Barzani, sustained serious head injuries and has been airlifted to an American air force base in Germany for specialist treatment.

Another 44 Kurds, many of them in serious condition, were taken to local hospitals for treatment. Reports that four American soldiers who had been escorting Commander Barzani were also killed in the so-called "blue-on-blue" incident could not be immediately confirmed.

The incident appears to be have been the result of mistaken targeting by American fighter pilots who had been called in by ground forces and were attempting to bomb an Iraqi tank column that had appeared over a ridge about three kilometres southwest of the bombed site.

The bomb landed in the centre of an intersection where the convoy of about 11 jeeps had arrived only minutes earlier as guests of Commander Barzani, who had invited a group of international reporters to accompany him on a visit to the front line.

The target, however, was another intersection, which from the air would probably look identical to, and thus could easily have been mistaken for, the correct target.

The incident happened at 12.30 p.m. near the village of Dibaga, where a fierce front-line fire fight between the Iraqis, who not long before had moved back a few kilometres, and the Americans, who had pushed forward, was in progress.

The scene on the road, which cuts through fields rich with the yellow flowers of oil seed plants, was transformed into one of utter devastation.

Pools of blood scarred the surface and clearly identifiable body parts were scattered amongst the smoking hulks of burned vehicles.

Splayed around a massive crater in the centre of the intersection were the twisted metal wrecks of seven or eight jeeps, the paint peeled off by the heat of the bomb blast.

"It was an ocean of fire," said Mr Abdullah Rahman, the commander of the 2nd peshmerga battalion. "People were screaming, screaming for help."

Mr Simpson, the world affairs editor of the BBC, received light shrapnel wounds and was able to broadcast from the site. His translator, Kamaran Abdurazaq Muhamed (25), was severely injured and died in an ambulance on the way to hospital. (Irish Times, April 7, 2003)

April 7 (Day 19)

How to describe this day? From 8 a.m. continuous bombing all over the place, very heavy bombing far away but as if it's over us.

Baghdad is in a terrible state. The pictures we see are awesome.

3 p.m. It's quiet for now but there is still an air raid in progress.

Air raids continuous all night, two massive cracks, one at about 10.30 p.m., which carried on sporadically through the night.

April 8 (Day 20)

THE COALITION OF THE WILLING: FACTS AND FIGURES

'We now have a coalition of the willing that includes some 30 nations' – Secretary of State Colin Powell

Now up to 47! Our 12 latest allies are: Costa Rica, Dominican Republic, Honduras, Iceland, Marshall Islands, Micronesia, Mongolia, Palau, Rwanda, Solomon Islands, Tonga and Uganda!

NATION	Per capita GDP (1)	Mil. expenditures as % of GDP (1) (in $B)	Annual amount spent on military	Troops in coalition (2, 3)	$ allocated in latest US budget (4)
Afghanistan	$800	NA	NA	0	127M
Albania	$3,800	1.49	0.056	70	
Australia	$24,000	2	9.3	2000	
Azerbaijan	$3,100	2.6	0.121	0	
Bulgaria	$6,200	2.7	0.356	150*	
Colombia	$6,300	3.4	3.3	0	34M
Costa Rica	$8,500	1.6	69	0	
Czech Rep.	$15,300	2.1	1.19	1 NBC* team	15M
Denmark	$29,000	1.4	2.47	1 sub, 1 warship	
Dom. Rep.	$5,800	1.1	.18	PW†	
El Salvador	$4,600	0.7	0.112	0	
Eritrea	$740	19.8	0.138	0	
Estonia	$10,900	2	0.155	0	
Ethiopia	$700	12.6	0.8	0	
Georgia	$3,100	0.59	0.023	0	
Honduras	$2,600	0.6	0.035	0	
Hungary	$12,000	1.75	1.08	0	$15M
Iceland	$27,100	0.9	0	0	
Italy	$24,300	1.64	20.2	0	
Japan	$27,200	1	40.7	0	
South Korea	$18,000	2.8	12.8	0	
Latvia	$7,800	1.2	0.087	Still deciding	
Lithuania	$7,600	1.9	0.23	0	
Macedonia	$4,400	6	0.2	0	
Micronesia	$2,000	NA	NA	0‡	
Netherlands	$25,800	1.5	6.5	360	
Nicaragua	$2,500	1.2	0.026	0	
Palau	$9,000	NA	NA	0¶	

Philippines	$4,000	1.5	0.995	PW†	
Poland	$8,800	1.71	3.5	200**	15M
Portugal	$18,000	2.2	1.2	0	
Romania	$6,800	2.47	0.985	278*	
Slovakia	$11,500	1.89	0.406	0	4.5M††
Spain	$20,700	1.15	8.6	1 medical ship	
Solomon Islands	$1,700	NA	NA	0	
Tonga	$2,200	NA	NA	0	
Turkey	$6,700	4.5	8.1	0	1B
Ukraine	$4,200	1.4	.5	500*	
UK	$24,700	2.32	31.7	45,000	
Uzbekistan	$2,500	2	0.2	0	
USA	$36,300	3.2	396	300,000	

* Nuclear, Biological, Chemical decontamination experts

† Undisclosed number of troops pledged for post-war deployment

** Non-combat troops

¶ Between 20 and 200 of Palau's 20,000 citizens reportedly already members of the U.S. military

‡ Micronesia is, by treaty, wholly dependent on the US for its defense.

†† Same amount was offered to Slovenia, which is NOT part of the coalition.

1 *CIA World Factbook*

2 AP wire service story

3 From the *National Post* (Canadian)

4 Reuters wire service report

Source: www.AReporter.com

Again banging now and again. The weather is very bad, perhaps this will give us a bit of space. The electricity is off and on, and the water is barely a trickle. To me this is the sign of the start of the things to come in Mosul.

We see from the TV the fighting in Baghdad and the houses in Monsoor after the four 2,000-lb bombs were dropped on them.

This is and was known by the Americans as a residential area. What justification do they have to carry out this kind of behaviour? I watch from Syrian TV three American soldiers pushing a middle-aged man to the floor. You can tell he is frightened because he can't understand them and all he is saying is: "Okay, okay." Is this the liberation they talk about?

Heavy fighting in Baghdad, and at the Kindi Hospital they have no power or water, no medical supplies.

The Americans have hit the Palestine Hotel in Baghdad with a tank, blowing a massive hole in the side of the building, killing a cameraman and injuring many others. And all they say is sorry.

April 9 (Day 21)

Heavy bombing all morning and afternoon. I've seen some amazing pictures from Baghdad. Bombing very heavy all afternoon. Pictures on TV show people dancing in the streets.

Bad night. Missiles flying and cracking all the time.

A curfew was enforced – 8 a.m. to 10 p.m. Things are very bad.

April 10 (Day 22)

8 a.m. A few missiles flying over but everything seems to be peaceful. We are all stressed out and tired. Yesterday, we were eating ice cream whilst bombs dropped all over – seems really weird. What a story we will tell when this is over. My kids just want to see their grandma; it's 15 years since they saw her.

2.30 p.m. From the TV and radio we learn that the Kurds have taken Kirkuk; that leaves Mosul and Tikrit.

My friend is very depressed and I try to cheer her up, take one day at a time, but I don't think it did her any good.

People looting from now. Kurds on the outskirts of Mosul just waiting. Had a quiet night. I think this is the beginning of the end.

April 11 (Day 23)

Liberation Day

Free at last. People are burning pictures all over the place. The G. building and hospital are gone, everything. We just want to be left alone. My friend is upset, her husband is in the Party and she is very worried for him. She has left her house. I think that was a mistake.

There is looting and burning widespread, it's awful. (My friend has lost her car.) They say there is fighting in the centre of Mosul between idiots and Kurdish forces.

MOSUL JOINS THE IRAQI DESCENT INTO MAYHEM ON A FRENZIED DAY OF LOOTING AND REVENGE

Anarchy and looting enveloped Mosul yesterday after Saddam Hussein's forces disappeared and the people reclaimed the ancient Iraqi city. At a branch of the Iraqi Central Bank, torn banknotes bearing the face of the vanished dictator littered the ground as frenzied groups of men smashed windows to get in and then carried away wads of the near-worthless cash. Shots rang out as Armalite rifles abandoned by fleeing Iraqi soldiers were carried off by jubilant, but lawless, young men who fired them into the air. Men, women and children ransacked offices of Mr Hussein's Ba'ath Party, loading everything they could into their cars, on to donkey carts, the backs of bicycles or slung over their shoulders.

"We are repeating what Saddam did to us. He took money from the people. Now we're taking some of it back," said Qusay Fouzi, 24. He pushed a cart along the boulevard by the Tigris River and proudly pointed out the three office chairs, glass-topped desk and two printers he had just looted from a state-run cement company.

American Special Forces moved into the city accompanied by Kurdish peshmerga militia at 4pm. They took over the central government building to set up a central command and ordered Kurdish militia to fan out around the city to bring the looting under control.

Within 15 minutes the Americans came under fire and pulled out of the city centre with one casualty.

The descent into chaos in Mosul came a day after the peshmerga swept unopposed into the nearby oil-rich town of Kirkuk, surprising their American supporters and alarming a Turkish government obsessed with preventing anything remotely resembling a de facto Kurdish state from emerging.

The violence is also just part of Iraq's terrifying descent into anarchy since Baghdad fell on Wednesday. American and Kurdish control over the two northern cities will aid the advance on Mr Hussein's Ba'athist and clan power base of Tikrit.

The euphoria that seemed to accompany the free-for-all in Mosul was not shared by all. Outside the Central Bank, medical student Alim Mohammed, 18, shook his head and expressed shame in his countrymen. "We need a system here, there is no law and order. The people are upset, they are desperate. But there is no one to bring us security," he said.

There was also some confusion about exactly what had happened to the 80,000 Ba'athist troops who had been preparing the city for an assault by the coalition forces for the past three weeks. Residents said that by early yesterday it was obvious that the regime's support had dissolved, as it had appeared to do across the northern front. "They disappeared in a moment," Mr Alim said. "One minute they were here and the next minute they were not."

At the offices of the Ba'athist Secret Service, the Mukhabarat, which had been badly damaged by bombs dropped by the Americans, people sifted through documentation, searching for the names of informants. Ferah Harki picked up a sheaf of paper from among the roses and rubble in the front garden and said he had found the names of people from his tribe – the Harki – who had become supporters of the regime and were now considered traitors of the clan. (South China Morning Post, *April 12, 2003)*

April 12 (Day 24)

A pretty quiet day. No water or electricity. They say there is looting all over Mosul.

A peaceful day but the night was awful, a gun battle outside my house between people who are guarding us – one group thought the other was looting. The place is in a state of anarchy.

April 13 (Day 25)

God Bless Mary, we love and miss you very much.

On this day two years ago, my dear younger sister died on Easter Friday after a long battle with cancer. I can't imagine my mum, what state she is in, there isn't a day goes by when Mary is not with me.

These last three weeks, I kissed her picture and she kept me going. I hadn't seen her for 12 years because of the sanctions and in August of 2000 my mum rang me and told me she had only a short time left to live. With special permission it took me four weeks before I could even leave Iraq. With no money, and nowhere to stay, I went by car to Jordan by myself. I left my family here. When I arrived I was taken into the house of a Jordanian student who had studied in Mosul. The most amazing and generous family. I am in debt for their kindness for the rest of my life. I went to the British Embassy and told them I needed to leave straight away. The Ambassador made me wait nine days before issuing me a new passport just because my husband was from Iraq. They say they want to help the Iraqis. I hope that woman will be judged for her actions and that God will forgive her, because I won't.

They say American soldiers are controlling the looting and some shops are opening. There is no petrol, no electricity, no water. We can hear and see artillery fire. It seems very close. I think it is all a bloody mess.

The Americans have entered the city of Tikrit. This should be something to see. I just want to find a phone or someone from the Red Cross to telephone my mum.

April 14 (Day 26)

A very peaceful day, quiet. Ali went to the hospital, found someone who had a phone. I will go with him tomorrow.

Good night, even watched a film on Syrian TV.

April 15 (Day 27)

This has been one to remember. I went to the hospital and I was so lucky. There were three journalists. A Dutchman named Aart, and a married couple, Lynne O'Donnell and her husband Damien. They are based in Turkey and had come to Mosul via Irbil. Lynne works for the *Irish Times* and her husband for the *Sunday Telegraph*. They let me use their phone and I rang my Mama. She was howling in sorrow. I have never heard her cry like that, but joy soon took over.

Then they talked to me and my son, and they asked him to go with them. He felt embarrassed but my daughter went for the day to translate. She was over the moon and showed them all over Mosul and talked to many people.

They paid her a salary – she told them she didn't want any payment, just the experience, but they insisted. They went to the airport in Mosul, she saw the American soldiers, she said they were over-powering.

They left my house at about 5 p.m. They said there had been trouble in the governor's building and the Americans had shot some people.

Mosul, Iraq (AFP) – At least 10 people were killed and scores wounded in the northern Iraqi city of Mosul when US troops fired on a crowd angered by a speech by the new US-backed governor, witnesses reported.

The charges were denied by a US military spokesman in the city Tuesday, who said troops had first come under fire from at least two gunmen and fired back, without aiming at the crowd.

But the incident overshadowed the start of US-brokered talks aimed at sketching out the country's future leadership in the southern city of

Nasiriyah, a Shiite Muslim bastion where 20,000 people marched through the city chanting "No to America, No to Saddam."

The fire fight in Mosul broke out as the newly-appointed governor of the city was making a speech from the building housing his offices which listeners deemed was too pro-US, witnesses said.

"There were protesters outside, 100 to 150, there was fire, we returned fire," a US military spokesman said, adding the initial shots came from a roof opposite the building, about 75 metres away.

"We didn't fire at the crowd, but at the top of the building," the spokesman added. "There were at least two gunmen, I don't know if they were killed. The firing was not intensive but sporadic, and lasted up to two minutes."

But witnesses charged that US troops fired into the crowd after it became increasingly hostile towards the new governor, Mashaan al-Juburi.

"They (the soldiers) climbed on top of the building and first fired at a building near the crowd, with the glass falling on the civilians. People started to throw stones, then the Americans fired at them," said Ayad Hassun, 37.

"Dozens of people fell," he said, his own shirt stained with blood.

"The people moved toward the government building, the children threw stones, the Americans started firing," another witness, Marwan Mohammed, 50, told AFP.

According to a third witness, Abdulrahman Ali, 49, the US soldiers opened fire when they saw the crowd running at the government building.

An AFP journalist saw a wrecked car in the square and ambulances ferrying wounded people to hospital, while a US aircraft flew over the northern city at low altitude.

A doctor at the city hospital, Ayad al-Ramadhani, said: "There are perhaps 100 wounded and 10 to 12 dead."

The process of finding a new Iraqi leadership after the fall of Iraqi leader Saddam Hussein got underway in Nasiriyah, the first meeting of opposition groups since the launch of the war on March 20, with US officials expected to discuss the process of forming an interim adminis-tration.

But the man tipped to become Iraq's next leader, Ahmad Chalabi, head of the US-backed Iraqi National Congress, was not due to attend.

Iraq's leading Shiite Muslim opposition group was also boycotting the talks, amid distrust over the US role and division over who should lead Iraq.

Chalabi, who has insisted he is not a candidate for a post in the interim administration to be run by retired US general Jay Garner, planned to send a representative.

Dozens of representatives from Iraq's fractious mix of ethnic, tribal and opposition groups, including those formerly in exile, were said to be invited although no official list was given.

The New York Times quoted Garner as saying his mission to rebuild Iraq's political structures would be messy and contentious.

His fears appeared justified as the talks in the Shiite bastion sparked a demonstration estimated by journalists to number around 20,000 people, led by religious figures.

April 16 (Day 28)

Nothing to report after yesterday. A demonstration ended in fighting and looting on a small scale. Three died, and seven injured.

April 17 (Day 29)

Busy trying to get straight. Mosul is calm. Another good day. The electricity is coming, but still no water.

April 18 (Day 30)

A beautiful day. The two reporters came. They had lunch and I sent for Margaret and we all had a good natter. I phoned my mum, and Margaret phoned Alia. There were plenty of tears.

They left about 4.30 p.m. They were going to Irbil, and then in the morning to Dohuk. We were very happy.

April 19 (Day 31)

A photographer who worked for Lynne came with a driver in a TV car and took some beautiful photos in the house and garden, even the dog got a look-in. He spent about 20 minutes with us. It was very special for us. The kids were thrilled.

9

The Lost City

At the time of writing, Mosul is a lost city. The people are shadowed by fear. The streets are battlegrounds where terrorists, zealots, insurgents and American soldiers fight for fleeting control. The collateral damage of innocent bystanders mounts daily. Car bombs are routine, snipers ubiquitous. Attack helicopters hover low overhead, tanks roar through the streets stopping for nothing. Automatic gunfire provides a staccato backbeat to the muezzin's call to prayer. Mosul has come to resemble that futuristic city of our nightmares – no law; no security; every man for himself.

Few residents bother any more to count the daily car bombs, most of which go unreported. ("A friend told me that even before twelve o'clock yesterday there were five explosions near the university," Pauline told me one April morning.) Some are so huge they incinerate entire blocks, blow the windows out of buildings for hundreds of metres, and leave behind bodies charred beyond recognition. Many people no longer venture from the sanctuary of their homes. A curfew empties the streets by ten o'clock every night, and the bridges linking the eastern and western sectors of the city over the Tigris are open only for an hour in the morning and an hour in the afternoon. Sometimes, the bridges are shut for days on end. Those who can afford it employ bodyguards who accompany them everywhere and even take their children to school. Few people have not been touched by the scourge of kidnapping that is now the principal activity of a criminal underworld terrorizing the city. The gangs work on information sold to them by the victims' friends, colleagues or associates, a post-Saddam version of the informant networks in which almost everyone in the country spied on everyone else and was, in turn, spied upon. These days, tribal leaders, gangsters and fanatics have harnessed that flow of information for their own, narrower ends. In this demoralizing, dehumanizing atmosphere, in which community trust has disintegrated, people are isolated from each other by fear and hate.

On April 20, 2006, a United Nations-affiliated news agency reported that 20,000 people, mostly women and children, had been kidnapped nationwide since the start of the year. That figure, astounding in its implication, comes from a survey conducted by 125 non-government organizations and so probably understates the true scale of the scourge. Criminal gangs "with different aims" were blamed. Extortionists were giving way to religious fanatics in the barbarity stakes.

Mosul's mobile phone networks and the Internet are often cut for days or weeks. Grenades are regularly tossed into Internet cafés and barber shops. Electricity is rare, barely a few hours a day. Those who can afford gasoline for generators are subject to erratic and expensive supply. Armed religious gangs forced some fuel distributors to cut prices so low they could no longer buy in supplies. Shortages are chronic. Gas cylinders for cooking are so prized that housewives hide them from thieves who come in the night. In the country that sits on a sea of oil, petrol splutters erratically from commercial pumps and people must queue for hours or even days to fill their tanks. Roadside black marketeers, whose one-gallon plastic jerry cans are filled with petrol of varying quality, are the chief source. On the street, petrol costs 25,000 dinars, or about US$15 a gallon. For those people with connections, and access to government coupons, the price drops to 6,000 dinars, or US$4, a gallon.

With the fall of the Ba'ath Party and the end of the first phase of the war, Mosul was engulfed by looting and anarchy, no different to that in many Iraqi cities, its population lost in an orgy of revenge for the decades of Saddam's brutality. With no significant American military presence, and no central authority, the city became a seething danger zone. Sonic boom flyovers by US military jets and intimidating aerobatics by Sikorsky helicopters aimed at cowering the populace to American control – using the rotors much as a nineteenth-century headmaster might have swished his cane to bring unruly charges to heel – were largely useless because the Marines just didn't have the manpower to back them up. By the time the 101st Airborne, under the command of General David Petraeus, arrived more than ten days after Mosul's fall, the authority vacuum had been filled where it really mattered: at street level.

Opposition to the occupation here, formerly a Saddam military stronghold, was strong and the insurgency quickly showed its intentions. Petraeus was one of the few US commanders in Iraq who came with experience of post-war situations (Haiti; Bosnia). He set about rebuilding the local government structures, re-employing bureaucrats, getting money flowing to pay salaries, and trying to imbue a sense of empowerment among decision-makers by introducing democratic processes at executive level. But with no police force, law and order remained elusive and Mosul became a multilayered city. As a newly imposed upper-echelon bureaucracy worked closely with the Americans, gangs consolidated control over the grass roots. Some were small-time thugs who extorted cash which they blew partying over the border in Syria. Some were underworld organizations growing in power, with access to networks of informers and able to effectively target families, professionals and businessmen they believed could pay substantial ransoms. Still others were linked to Islamists, and newly formed groups of former soldiers raising cash to fund an anti-occupation insurgency. Sandwiched between an ineffectual government and the increasingly effective criminal orders were a couple of million Moslawis, their early hopes for a brighter future fading fast.

Mosul's slide below the parapet of civilized existence has gone generally unremarked by the outside world, which views the news through the prism of Iraq as a concept and Baghdad as its manifestation. High-profile incidents in the city – such as the massive battle in July, 2003, that ended in the killing of Saddam Hussein's sons, Uday and Qusay – have generated international headlines. But the car bomb that destroyed a row of shops, including the boutique owned by Pauline's son-in-law, doesn't even make a statistical reckoning. Nor does the one that exploded a block from Margaret's home, so huge it blew out all the windows in her house. Nor those five before midday near Mosul University one fine April morning in 2006, more than three years after the invasion that had been billed as Operation Iraqi Freedom.

Al Qaeda militants flooded into Iraq from elsewhere in the region in the months immediately after President Bush told Americans, on May 1, 2003, that the mission in Iraqi had been accomplished – that Iraqis were now free. "Bring 'em on," he later said of the terrorist organizations that transformed Iraq into a theatre of violence. As they grew in number, so they grew in strength, and their public atrocities – beheadings, point-blank assassinations, roadside bombs – fomented widespread fear that added to their power and confidence. Evidence began to mount that they were teaming up with former soldiers of Saddam's army to launch military-style assaults. By late 2004, many disparate anti-occupation groups had united into a movement that was able to coordinate attacks and take control of entire cities and regions – Fallujah, Najaf, Ramadi, Samarra and, briefly in late 2004, Mosul.

It happened while American military attention was focused on Fallujah, a small town not far from Baghdad where the foreign-led terrorist forces had control and were using it as a base for training fighters and launching assaults on US forces and other perceived enemies. The US military planned an assault on the town aimed at wiping out the insurgency, and spent weeks amassing thousands of troops close by, somewhat diminishing the element of surprise. While international media with journalists "embedded" with the troops were beaming their reports of the assault build-up the world over, the insurgents were making preparations of their own. By the time the Americans moved on Fallujah, after the US presidential election had secured a second term for George W. Bush, most of the city's 300,000 residents had left, encouraged by the coalition authorities to evacuate.

Presented with the opportunity to leave the town under the noses of the troops sent in to Fallujah to eliminate them, many of the insurgents evacuated, too, joining the flood of traumatized residents and, incognito, heading to nearby Ramadi and to Mosul, hundreds of miles away in the north. Here they regrouped and, in coordinated attacks on police stations across Mosul, they made off with arms, ammunition, cars, radios and police uniforms. More than 70 per cent of Mosul's 4,000 policemen – trained at great cost to the American taxpayer – panicked in the face of the onslaught and deserted, or simply switched sides. Those who stayed on were ordered to remain indoors because troops could not be sure that anyone in a police uniform was not an insurgent. The militants had bombs, rocket-propelled grenades, automatic rifles and at least one anti-aircraft gun that was fired on a convoy of US armoured vehicles. Insurgents turned streets into shooting galleries as small sniper teams took up positions on rooftops along streets the American convoys had to pass through.

The Americans called in air strikes and began bombing. In mid-November, almost three thousand American and Iraqi troops massed for a counter-offensive that lasted days. As had happened earlier, in Fallujah, and has happened so often since, the coalition appears to have been able to retake the city only because the militants stopped fighting. Once the combat was over, the dirty war began. Bodies, sometimes ten or more at a time, turned up every few days, often decapitated – police, security guards, men who worked with the city and provincial governments. Politicians, and their bodyguards, were murdered. Christians, too, were kidnapped, killed or forced to flee. While authorities in Baghdad, Washington and London were trenchantly denying that the situation in Iraq was approaching civil war, the locals were just getting on with it.

By now, both the criminal and Islamist gangs marauding through Mosul neighbourhoods were becoming selective. Methodology had been refined – a phone call or, more often, a letter under the gate of an intended victim's home stating the cost of not being kidnapped, usually tens of thousands of dollars – and specific targets singled out, principally among the professional classes: doctors, lawyers, judges, teachers, pharmacists, accountants, academics, merchants. Hard-working people, more often than not with one breadwinner in the family, their only assets a house and a car, and like the middle classes the world over, with little cash to spare.

Almost all Mosul's doctors have been driven out by threats. The head of the provincial council of Nineveh, Salim al-Haj Essa, said in May, 2006, that nine Mosul doctors had been killed in the previous three months, and, in the same period, 66 doctors had left the city for their own safety after receiving demands for large amounts of cash so that they and their families could remain free and alive. He blamed criminal gangs, and said some arrests had been made. "But [we] discovered that the head of one of these networks worked as a hospital guard," he said. A hospital guard, a gatekeeper to more than the premises; just the thought sends shards of icy panic through Pauline and Ali. The guards at Ali's hospital have access to information about where the doctors live, how many children they have and where they go to school, what time the doctors come to work, what time they leave, what route they take home, what cars they drive. Every morning and evening they wave hello and goodbye to the doctors as they come and go. They occupy positions of trust, but they clearly cannot be trusted.

A month earlier, Pauline had told me that in the space of just one week fifteen medical professionals – doctors, laboratory technicians, pathologists – had packed up their families and left, heading from the fear of Mosul into the protected, and effectively closed, Kurdish region, or abroad to Syria and Jordan. "They want money to buy arms to fight the Americans," Pauline said of the gangs driving the doctors out. "It's not a Sunni–Shia thing, it's just the 'resistance.' This is what they have been doing all the time. They go so long and then they run out of money and it starts again. It's terrible. Two friends of ours were threatened, geologists who don't have anything, they just happen to work at the university. He was asked for ten thousand dollars and gave a thousand, all he had."

Soon after, Mosul's doctors, surgeons, pharmacists, lab technicians, even lecturers in the medical departments at the university, were so exasperated and exhausted by the unrelenting persecution that they took to the streets, marching to demand that the authorities give them protection. Then they went on strike. Many failed to return to their hospitals, universities and clinics. Mosul's health facilities – once among the best in the country, built on people like Ali, trained abroad and with an earnest respect for their Hippocratic oath – have all but disappeared. Medicines, already in short supply as distribution networks had dissolved, have largely run out. "No polio vaccine, no diphtheria or whooping cough vaccine, no anaesthetic for operations, nothing," Pauline said. What medicines were available were prohibitively expensive.

Essa admitted that the impact on public health of the kidnapping campaign, which his council was powerless to curtail, was devastating. "Patients, especially victims of terrorist attacks, receive shabby treatment," he said. During the last months of her second pregnancy, Pauline's daughter received no pre-natal medical care because she couldn't find an obstetrician. All the clinics had closed. A family friend who worked at a hospital began stockpiling things that would be needed when Noor gave birth – sterile gloves, swabs, even clamps for the umbilical cord. There were no guarantees that, when the time came, any of these basic items would be available.

Once the ranks of Mosul's academics, doctors, lawyers and judges had been decimated, gangs turned on merchants. Supermarket or market stall, nothing was too big or too small for the extortionists. Even those traders who had been paying protection money for years found the price on their heads had gone up. Shops were blown up, shopkeepers and their relatives kidnapped and killed. After the kidnap, torture and murder of the ten-year-old son of a local trader in early 2006, shops in the centre of the city began to close and shopowners took their children out of school. Another layer of Mosul's historic civility was disappearing. Soon, it will scarcely matter as the crooks and hoodlums will have no one to turn on but each other – and the poor and terrified who have nowhere to run.

There had been a moment when Mosul looked as if it would be the success story of the new Iraqi order. Once General Petraeus moved in, he made some friends among senior community figures and distributed millions of dollars to buy – some would say rent – the loyalty and cooperation that made his programmes look credible. In late 2003 and early 2004, Petraeus was popular in the American media for his level-headed approach, his Ivy League education and his ability to do more push-ups than men a third of his age. News media especially liked the small touches, such as the signs he posted in barracks reading: "What have you done to win Iraqi hearts and minds today?" and "We are in a race to win over the people." Thanks to Petraeus's determination, the newspapers and magazines said, Mosul was among the first places to hold local elections. His penchant for doling out cash had helped kick-start many small, localized projects that helped create jobs. "Money is ammunition," the general told one reporter.

The media were desperate for good news from Iraq and Petraeus fitted the image of a hero. Few residents seemed able to see things in quite the same way. The mantra from Pauline and Margaret was one of spiralling hopelessness, which began with criminal opportunists and descended into sectarian terrorism. At election time, there were factional gunfights in the streets. The polling booth in the school opposite Pauline's home became campaign HQ for Islamist ruffians whose only platform was to ensure no one voted. The reality and the rhetoric just didn't gel. Hope needs a reason to live, and Mosul's residents, for the most part, were offered no incentive for keeping their hopes alive.

The spiral coiled tighter. Efforts at regenerating basic civil services were thwarted by the insurgency, and as long as electricity, water and telecommunications failed to work, people blamed the Americans. Efforts to get oil wells and refineries working so the country could start earning desperately needed foreign exchange were thwarted by insurgency attacks, yet as long as there were no jobs the people blamed the Americans. The insurgency attacks on the Americans became bolder, forcing them on to the defensive, further isolating them from ordinary Iraqis. Attacks on foreigners who brought expertise, initiative and funding to get industry working again grew more violent, so fewer came and even less got done. Men who joined the national police and army were killed in ever greater numbers, and those left behind couldn't be trusted, so fewer risked signing up. With no local security forces, criminal violence spilled into vigilantism and warlordism. Resentment of the hamstrung American occupation as a cause of the violence became its excuse. The daily rhythm of life is controlled by criminals, jihadis, insurgents and terrorists who have created a terrorized state that rivals, perhaps even surpasses, the tyranny of Saddam Hussein.

Saleh has lived in the house next door to Pauline for most of his life. He is in his late sixties, has eleven children, and buried his wife five years before the Allied invasion. His greatest pleasures in life were his friends and his garden. Each morning and evening, he would do as elderly men in Mosul have been doing since time immemorial – he would sit out on his front step sharing gossip and tea with his old neighbours. Until he was told not to. The message was passed on by someone he didn't know, who offered no reason, just an implied consequence for non-compliance. Saleh no longer sits on his step to sip chai and chat with his friends. And his garden has grown to weeds. He stays indoors, frightened of what and of whom he isn't sure.

Saleh's eldest son, Khalid, was also approached by a "concerned citizen," who, without explanation, told him to stop his regular trips to Dohuk, over the former line of control and into the Kurdish area, to buy vegetables. He'd spent fifteen years in Iran after being taken prisoner at the front during the Iran–Iraq War. After being freed from a PoW camp, he'd stayed in Iran, afraid of what would happen to him if he returned to Saddam's Iraq. Saddam had murdered his generals for poor battlefield performances; what would he do to an enlisted man who had been taken prisoner and then dared return? Once the coast seemed clear, Khalid came home, with his Iranian wife and their children, and went into business for himself, driving every couple of days to Dohuk, paying wholesale prices for vegetables imported from Turkey, and selling them at a stall he rented in one of Mosul's main markets. Soon, the market became dangerous, a magnet for shakedown men, kidnappers and bombers. So Khalid began selling his vegetables to local grocers – the quality of the produce was better and the prices lower than anything Mosul market gardeners could offer, so business was good. Until the message came – no more trips to Dohuk to buy vegetables.

These warnings don't come at the end of a gun, and the source is never identified. But the message is clear – we are watching you; we don't like what we see; if you don't stop, we'll kill you.

Like most Moslawis, Saleh and Khalid have left the dictatorship of Saddam behind, wishing it good riddance. But now they live in a society terrorized by the anonymous, for reasons they cannot be sure of. Their every action becomes a calculation of life and death. Every movement is as likely to be watched as it was in Saddam's day, but now with unknowable, unimaginable consequences. There is no respite. There is no point in going to police who cannot be trusted because there is no law. Hardworking people are bullied and exploited with impunity. Behaviour that in a normal city would be cheered as entrepreneurial here carries a death sentence. Why? Why can't Khalid go to Dohuk to buy vegetables that people in Mosul want to buy? Is it because Dohuk is a Kurdish town, and Mosul's Arabs shouldn't be supporting the Kurds, who many regard as beneficiaries of the decades of war and sanctions? Is it an internecine Islamic thing – Mosul Shia versus Kurdish Sunni? Was it for his own safety, a warning that would keep him off dangerous roads? Is it the psychopathic behaviour of street thugs and racketeers? Is there any point in even wondering whether the warning comes from jihadis, foreign militants, tribal rivals, adherents of the former regime fighting the good fight against the Kurds, or a community-minded mosque-goer whose well-meaning advice is delivered a little too enthusiastically?

Every second of every day entails precaution and forethought. In Saddam's Iraq, insane as it was, people generally felt safe on the streets and in their homes. Not any more. In Saddam's Iraq, as degraded as it became after decades of war and international sanctions, for the most part the water flowed, the lights came on, the phones worked and there was enough petrol to keep the family car on the road. Not any more. Today the people of Mosul are yoked by another tyranny, but this one goes by the name of freedom.

10

"They called me
Mother of the Tribe"

Margaret's life began unravelling almost immediately the war ended. It came apart in ways that were not officially supposed to happen. Iraq's new rulers took over Saddam's bastion – soon to become infamous as the Green Zone – promising an era of inclusive and democratic government. Margaret's family soon discovered that the administration was nothing of the sort.

"There's going to be a witch hunt," she had said when we met, just after the city's fall. "You mark my words." What she hadn't told me was that the payback for her husband's decades of government service had already begun. In the midst of the looting, Margaret and Zuhair had taken the boys to the al-Sharook family compound in the old centre of town, where, behind the high stone walls, they knew they would be safe from the escalating turmoil. While they were gone, Zuhair's car, which was part of the university's pool and had blue government licence plates, was stolen from their garage, and the thieves left signs of having tried to enter the house, too. Every government car on their estate, which had a couple of hundred houses for university staff, had been stolen that same night. Senior faculty, like the president, the dean and heads of department, all had the same sedans as Zuhair with the same telltale blue plates. "All went that night, except one," Margaret said. "That one was too far down the end of the estate and they had hidden it very well." The blatant rancour of the thievery, so direct and sudden, was an early indication of the vindictiveness that found outlet in the power games that were about to be played out between various politicized groups – as usual, ethnic, religious, tribal – with the hapless Americans, ignorant of the competing interests and old scores, as referee.

Zuhair held senior rank in the Ba'ath Party. He had been well educated by the state, gaining a doctorate in the United Kingdom, and becoming a professor of zoology at Mosul University. Having chosen to take his career into management, by the time Operation Iraqi Freedom overwhelmed his country he was one of the foremost tertiary educationists and administrators in Iraq. As president of Mosul University, a post he had assumed in 2002, he had opposed the war. As he watched the institution being stripped of everything from computers to plumbing in the days after the Americans entered the city, he refused to allow the foreign troops to provide security, believing their presence would cause further disruption and upset among the students. It was probably unfortunate that he'd gone on the record comparing the Americans to Hulagu's hordes, who had invaded and razed the city 600 years earlier – echoing Saddam's call before the Allied invasion for Iraqis to unite against the "new Mongols." As it was, Zuhair was the last man standing at the university, armed and ready to defend it from invader and looter alike.

Within about two months, Zuhair was sacked from his post, accused of failing to move with the times. His removal was high profile, reported by Western media, and appeared to contradict claims by the Coalition Provisional Authority that the presidents of Iraq's tertiary institutions had voluntarily stood down so that their faculty could re-elect them, or their replacements. Zuhair's dismissal, on May 15, 2003, came about with a unanimous vote by the newly installed Mosul City Council. Major General David H. Petraeus, the American in charge of the Nineveh region, called it "democracy in action." The city's new deputy mayor, Khasro Goran, said Zuhair had been removed because "we have a lot of reports from students and teachers that he still thinks in the old way."

Events in the weeks leading up to his formal dismissal were complicated and confusing. Zuhair, Margaret said, had been travelling often to Baghdad to meet with Jay Garner, Washington's first viceroy in Iraq, and discuss the immediate needs of the university. He and Garner apparently

*

got on well, and once Petraeus arrived in Mosul, Zuhair attempted to forge a similar relationship with him, based on mutual respect. But Margaret believes the Americans were naive and too easily manipulated when it came to doling out power to local interests. She watched as control of Mosul City Council went to members of religious parties who saw the fall of the Ba'ath as an opportunity to pay back the minority Sunni Muslims for decades of repression under Saddam. Zuhair, a secular Sunni, didn't stand a chance, Margaret says. "His name was blackened. I went to the Americans to try to explain what was going on, but by then it was too late. The Americans didn't understand the processes that were going on. The Islamis," as she calls those whose plan was to run things according to regressive, religious principles, "worked very hard to get on with the Americans so they could push their own agenda, and it worked for them. They got the council, and they got the university. There was no election at Mosul University. If there had been, Zuhair would have won."

There may be no way now to test the veracity of Margaret's faith in Zuhair's popularity; as it was, he lost his job and his position and was, for the first time in 30 years, unemployed. He was also unemployable, at least in Iraq. In neighbouring Jordan and Syria, where the authorities – typical of Arab and Muslim countries in the aftermath of the war – offered little support in bringing peace or stability to Iraq, Zuhair was unable to find work that suited his qualifications and financial needs. So, in late 2003, he moved to Yemen, to a post with the University of Ibb, as professor of physiology at the science college, where he taught dental students.

Margaret was left at home with her three boys, Ali, Omar and Taleb. It was, she says, the first time that she and Zuhair were really apart, not knowing when they would be together again as a couple and as a family. The elder twin, Ali, had been active in the student union of his college, but, perhaps tainted by the family association, he was soon pushed out by the religious forces that were gaining dominance. As the situation closed in on foreigners, Margaret's fears for the safety of her sons – easily identified as not quite Arab – intensified. As did questioning from family and friends about why she was staying in Iraq. She and the boys had their passports. They had travelled to the Green Zone in mid-2003, almost immediately the war was over, to get new British passports, as Saddam had long ago given foreigners the choice of either rescinding the nationality of their birth or leaving Iraq.

In mid-2005, missing her husband and knowing Mosul held no future she wanted for her sons, Margaret decided the time had come. Zuhair came home to Mosul and the planning began. As soon as Ali had completed his computer studies course and graduated, they packed him off on his own to Jordan, where he spent some time with his sister, Alia, and her family before flying to London and moving in with one of Margaret's brothers. Taleb talked his parents into letting him drop out of college, having realized he'd made a mistake in choosing to study food technology. ("Just not for me," he said later.) Omar wanted to finish his veterinary science degree, which meant another year at Mosul University. Reluctantly, Margaret said he could stay, and arranged for relatives to move into her house to look after him. And then she started to pack.

Just after dawn on September 9 or 10 – Margaret is not sure which – a white, six-seater GMC four-wheel-drive suburban sedan pulled up outside their house and they began loading it. "We had one suitcase each of our own things and a suitcase of linen and a few other things that we didn't think we could do without. I grabbed a few photos, my daughter's wedding album, a few old pictures of the family, and left everything else," she said. The end had finally arrived.

Margaret had hardly been out of the house for two years, making only brief and furtive, sanity-preserving trips to the shops on Nineveh and University streets in the company of her youngest sister-in-law, Luma, and her husband. Olive hadn't been out of her room, and hardly out of her bed, for the best part of a decade. Getting her from her first-floor bedroom, down the stairs, out through the front door and into the six-seater was one of the biggest challenges of the day. Olive is 5 foot 11 inches in her bare feet. It was a tight fit. Margaret had helped her mother into a full-length, embroidered dishdasha to cover her nightdress, and the three men

– Zuhair, Taleb and the taxi driver, an old friend of the family – helped support her towering frame as they were guided down the stairs in a slow-moving, gangling shuffle by Margaret, who was terrified they'd lose their balance and their grip, and come tumbling down the stairs towards her in a twisted tangle of broken arms and legs. Once outside, it was another task all together, as the no-longer-willowy Olive had to be carried from the front door of the house to the back door of the car, a matter of feet that felt like miles. The men huffed and puffed. Olive moaned and groaned. Margaret flitted up and down the path, glancing out at the road and around at the neighbouring houses, fearful that the commotion would draw unwelcome attention and blow the secrecy of their flight. Not even all of the immediate family knew they were leaving, subterfuge and deception being the friends of safety in the new Iraq.

Once they reached the car, Olive had to be wedged behind the middle seat, which Margaret pulled forward, and hoisted up on to the back seat, so she could lean her back against the opposite window and stretch her legs out on the seat in front of her. Margaret climbed in ahead of her mother. The driver had given up and was smoking a cigarette as he watched the elderly woman being manhandled, by Zuhair and Taleb, backwards into his car. Margaret leaned forward and hooked her arms under Olive's armpits and drew her mother back into the car's interior and up on to the seat. Zuhair lifted his mother-in-law's legs clear and, as if he was pushing a fragile wheelbarrow, gently guided her into the car, pushing as Margaret pulled. Bent double, he leaned into the car, still gripping Olive's ankles, as Margaret, kneeling in the space between the two seats, arranged a cushion behind Olive's back. Zuhair placed his mother-in-law's legs on the seat. Margaret tucked a blanket around them, patted Olive's hand and put a bedpan on the floor between the seats. God knew how they were going to deal with *that* when the time came.

As the adenoidal wails of the muezzins' calls for morning prayer began to reach their unsynchronized climax across the Mosul rooftops, Margaret, Zuhair and Taleb took their own places in the car – Margaret and Taleb in the middle, and Zuhair, smoking, up front with the driver. Margaret wore a full-length black abaya, the traditional, all-covering garb of the devout and demure Arab housewife, and a scarf over her hair. She didn't cover her face. She hid the three British passports – Olive's, Taleb's and her own – in the seat-belt stock. The sun was beginning its climb, the city's dusk-to-dawn curfew was coming to an end and the bridges were about to open. Before too many men began making their way from their beds to the mosques, the al-Sharooks, and Olive, took their leave of Mosul.

The next 24 hours passed like an out-of-body experience for Margaret. Adrenalin coursed through her veins, shortening her breath and clamping her back teeth so fast that her jaw ached for days after. Her scalp tingled and the skin between her shoulder blades crawled. Her head swam. Her eyes could barely focus, and she was hardly able to form coherent thoughts. At each roadblock, when men in blue shirts – with the feared "POLICE" insignia stitched on to the right sleeve – appeared at her window, her heart tightened and her stomach flipped over so violently she thought she would be ill. Her palms were sticky with perspiration, and rivulets of sweat trickled down the backs of her calves. In the front seat, Zuhair smoked; beside Margaret, to her right, Taleb gazed out of his window; in the back seat, Olive dozed. Margaret felt every minute as if it was an hour. She willed the car forward to freedom, true freedom, out of Iraq.

"The story was that I was going to Jordan on a holiday to see my daughter, and that I'd be coming back," Margaret told me when I met up with her in London a couple of months later. "It was awful. In some ways, I didn't want to leave the family. But I didn't have any choice, and many people couldn't leave even if they wanted to. I'd had two years at home, not being able to go out. Foreigners were being targeted. I was afraid. You just never knew what was going to happen, whether there would be a shoot-out and you'd get caught in the crossfire, or American spraying. I had to think of my sons' future."

Any sort of life had to be better than the one they were leaving behind, she remembered thinking as they passed through the Mosul Gate and turned on to the Mosul–Baghdad Highway, Route One, which would take them away from the daily terror of the New Iraq. To find that future she wanted for her family, Margaret had first to accompany them on one of the most dangerous trips in the world, on roads controlled either by American soldiers, the Ba'athist resistance, the religious insurgency or bandits. Encounters with any could end in death, though so far only Iraqis were torturing and decapitating their victims. The general wisdom, Zuhair said, was that "the Americans controlled the highways, the resistance controlled the rest." If you were held up, kidnapped, or worse, by bandits, then that was just bad luck. Margaret was prepared for a robbery: "I had a couple of gold rings and some money, in case we did get robbed, so I could just hand it over and hope for the best. It didn't happen, but that didn't stop me thinking all the time that it could happen."

As dawn turned to daylight, the car hit its rhythm and a tense, sad silence settled on the al-Sharooks. For the first couple of hours, before they reached the greasy, post-industrial town of Baiji, there was nothing to say. Each was lost in his or her own thoughts of what they'd left behind. Only Zuhair had a life outside Iraq – hardly an ideal existence in Yemen, thousands of miles from his wife and children. Margaret was regretting that she had not been able to say goodbye to the people she had lived among and loved for almost thirty years. "People did think it was inevitable I'd leave because I'm foreign; they thought I was stupid for staying and they'd say so all the time. In a nice way, of course. I was leaving my home, my things. I didn't know what the future would hold, if I'd go back, if I wouldn't go back. I was thinking about my relatives and friends, and if I'd see them again. And the children – I'd miss them growing up. I was upset. When you've lived with people for twenty-eight years, well, they're family, aren't they? And I couldn't say goodbye.

"They used to call me Ama Ashira – mother of the tribe. My husband is the oldest, and I was the oldest woman. So my house was the centre and I used to keep the family together. My house was open and, every Friday, everyone would come for lunch and bring a pan of food. All the way, as we were driving, I was thinking, have I done the right thing? Should I have stayed? But it was something I had to do – for my safety, to get my kids out, to make a future. We had to leave; there was no future there. And I knew that there wouldn't be for a long time. And my husband was not there. I'd been on my own for two years and there is nothing in Iraq for him now, so what's the point of staying? But I didn't know what I'd face when I got to London – would I find work? Would the boys find work?

"And, believe it or not, I was excited, too, because I was going to a new life. And I'd be able to speak my own tongue. It was very exciting. So there were two emotions. I had days leading up to our leaving when I was excited, and days when I was down about it. I was ready for a change."

This early in the day, there was little traffic on the highway as it descended from the foothills of the Kurdish mountains and on to the arid Arab plain. The verdant fertility of the northern breadbasket quickly gave way to unremittingly torpid brown flats that spread out endlessly on each side of the strip of black bitumen. Villages, set back a kilometre or two, had yet to stir. The rule of thumb on these roads is to train your eyes on the road ahead, avoid making eye contact with people in other vehicles, and hope that, while you're not looking at them, they're not looking at you. Margaret clutched her gold-ring ransom, and Zuhair assumed that his professorial manner could get them out of any trouble they might encounter with the locals. And then one of the most dreadful, and intractable, problems anyone travelling by road in Iraq can encounter appeared on the highway ahead: an American military patrol. A duo of massive armoured vehicles, the colour of the terrain, each with a machine gun atop, manned by a helmeted trooper. And going no faster than 25 miles an hour. After almost three years in Iraq, these guys had learned to shoot to kill anyone who came too close to their convoys. But how close was too close? Drivers are forced to calculate their own speeds, to monitor their distance from the Bradleys, or Strykers, or Humvees, while trying to make their own progress. And as the Americans occupy the entire road, often moving against the traffic, they create massive tailbacks that turn time into torture. Everyone feels like a sitting duck, vulnerable to attack by suicidal maniacs ready to ram random targets with cars loaded with high explosives. Convoys and checkpoints hold up drivers for hours. As Zuhair said: "If a soldier wants a piss, you have to stop for half an hour. You can't go near them, for fifty metres, or they shoot you. Because they're frightened. The Americans think that by threatening people they will make them stop supporting the resistance. But that's the Iraqi culture; they will always give support to their own."

At Baiji, the driver stopped for a bite at a taxi café famous for its food, and he hooked up with another driver, who had been hired to ferry a pair of priests along the same route to the Jordanian border. The drivers decided it would be safer for all if they travelled in convoy. So with the priests bringing up the rear, the al-Sharooks turned back on to Highway One for the second leg of the journey, only this time, between Baiji and the northernmost point of the Sunni Triangle at Samarra, they began taking short cuts, darting on to secondary roads to avoid the military convoys and jams on the highway, mainly around Tikrit. While the city is viewed as a Ba'athist stronghold, home of Saddam Hussein and the relatives he promoted to high office, it has remained relatively peaceful and secure since the end of the war, thanks to an assiduously negotiated pact between its former leaders and the American-led occupation forces. The grey and barren landscape around Tikrit, however, is a lawless no man's land of vigilantism and vengeance, where any approaching vehicle could be the last you ever see, and villages fire on strangers as a matter of course, viewing all outsiders as the enemy.

About 5 kilometres before Samarra, they turned off the sealed road and on to a sandy track that took them into the equally lawless hinterland around picturesque Tharthar Lake. It was as if they had swapped planets, leaving the dusty plane for a lush and reedy oasis. Narrow canals, lined with reeds taller than a man, course through this district. Most of the roads are little more than pounded pathways, many not wide enough for one car to pass another. The Americans don't come here. There is no way of knowing what, or who, is hidden in the foliage that flourishes along the sides of dirt roads that are certainly too narrow for their unwieldy vehicles. Many of the tracks are mined. Those that are passable are potholed from bombs; the roadsides are scattered with the burned-out shells of cars hit from the air by helicopter gunfire, or blown up from beneath by buried mines. "There were people fishing in a boat, there were gardens along the banks, the scenery was very beautiful, very green. But the road was terrible," Margaret said, remembering the juxtaposition of the father–son angling idyll, the floral canal banks and the remains of exploded cars. What had happened to the people in them? she'd wondered. This was a well-worn road, a popular short cut to Mosul as it cuts around 100 kilometres off the trip from the Jordan border, bypassing Baghdad, with its incessant roadblocks and checkpoints, by detouring through the Tharthar basin to the Fallujah Junction.

It was near the junction, as they were bearing down on the motorway that leads to the borders of Jordan and Syria, in the heart of the Sunni stronghold, with no Allied military presence to offer even the semblance of security to a carload of foreign passport-holders, that the driver announced they needed petrol. And so they joined a five-hour queue to buy fuel from the black marketeers who, all over Iraq, spend their days peddling petrol from jerry cans that stand in the scorching sun by the side of the road. "Scary," Margaret said, understating the extent of the danger of standing still in a country where every stranger is a potential murderer. "You don't know who these people are, who they are connected to, what their motives are. They could be bandits, see that you're a foreigner, and fifty kilometres up the road they come and rob you, or kidnap you. You don't have a choice, though, if you need petrol." The queue moved more slowly than a snail, edging forward one car-length at a time. And as the chilling awareness of the dire possibilities this interlude held for them began to descend on the other occupants of the car, Olive, bless her heart, opened her eyes and, not knowing where she was, nor understanding what was really going on, became a liability. For most of the day, she had been lying on the back seat, snoozing peacefully. Black curtains shielded her from the glare of the sun and the stares of suspicious eyes. With her head lolling against the back seat and her eyes softly shut, she seemed to have overcome the emotion of their pre-dawn departure and settled into the hum of the road. But just at the moment when the car was finally pulling up on the gravelled patch of roadside occupied by the petrol sellers, the nicotine cravings of a lifetime seemed to coalesce. Suddenly wide awake, Olive sat bolt upright, in the mood for a ciggie and a chat. Outside, the air shimmered with petrol fumes. Men in long, white dishdashas, chequered tribal scarves wound round their heads and falling over their shoulders, milled around with no obvious role, other than a close inspection of each car, and its occupants. Margaret panicked. She turned around to shush her mother. "She didn't really know what was going on or where we were or why we would have to be cautious, so she kept sitting up and chatting," Margaret said. "I kept trying to push her head down because we didn't want anyone to know that there were any foreigners in the car."

Olive had wept as the preparations for the family's departure gathered irreversible momentum. She'd joined Margaret in 1981, and apart from a short stint back in London in 1988 – when an Australian doctor had advised her to return to Iraq with the words: "Go on, get yourself some sunshine" – Mosul had been just as much her home as it had been Margaret's. When the twins were born, she said, "Ali was Margaret's baby and Omar was my baby." Margaret made sure that no matter what the circumstances, Olive had a daily paper (in Algiers she read the French newspapers with the help of a dictionary; in Iraq it was the English-language *Baghdad Observer*), an endless supply of cigarettes and a radio tuned to the BBC World Service. "The papers in Iraq were rubbish," Olive snorted. She consumed books, too, which along with bacon were at the top of her list of requests for anyone heading out of the country. When the rest of the family went over to Zuhair's mother's home for their Friday get-together, Olive would stay home and cook herself bacon, and then spend hours scouring the frying pan to scrub away any traces of evidence that she was secretly eating pork in a predominantly Muslim country.

She doesn't see her life in Mosul as having been anything other than normal. "You just got used to it," she told me. "It was the same as being in England, because we were at home. We looked after the kids, and we got on with things." Born on June 1, 1928, she was in her early fifties when she arrived in Iraq. Though many of the people she came into contact with spoke English because it was taught in the schools, nevertheless she learned the Arabic salutations and enough to make herself understood to the elderly al-Sharook aunts. "We had good friends," she remembered. "All nationalities."

As she got older and negotiating the stairs of the Mosul family home became more difficult, she said it just became easier to stay in her room. It was a refuge from the pressures of a war-racked society. She could sit by her window, listening to news of the outside world on her short-wave radio, smoking her cigarettes and watching the comings and goings of the household through the front gate down below. And when she did need to move – from bed to armchair to bathroom and back – she had her stick, or the steadying arm of a grandchild. And she was content.

Her earlier pluck did make a brief and useful return when the Ba'athist bureaucrats decided that she would have to leave the country to renew her resident's visa. By the mid-nineties, it wasn't really possible for Olive to go and stand in endless government department queues, filling in forms and getting them ticked and stamped by snotty, resentful clerks who might, or might not, send her off to do it again somewhere else. But that was what the local authorities in Mosul were insisting that she do. Olive decided that she'd write to the only man in the country who she believed was in a position to help. One afternoon, she sat up in her bed and with Margaret's help penned a letter to Saddam Hussein. "Dear Mr President," it began, and went on to explain, in intricate detail, Olive's history in Mosul, her family and her connections, via Zuhair, to the Ba'ath Party. She asked for his understanding and indulgence in allowing her to stay in Iraq, without having to jump through bureaucratic hoops every time her visa expired. Within a week, Saddam Hussein came through for Olive. She was granted an extension of her visa without having to leave the country, and was allowed automatic annual renewal, without having to leave her bed.

Ironically, when the family arrived at the border with Jordan, a nerve-shredding sixteen hours after their tearful departure from Mosul, Olive was not permitted to leave the country because she didn't have the requisite exit visa. Somehow, she had slipped through the bureaucratic cracks that had been opened by the 2003 war, and her name did not appear on the computer at the border passport control office as having been granted permission to leave. "They were going to send us back to Baghdad, to the immigration department, to try and get through the bureaucracy there," says Margaret, her astonishment at the officiousness of officialdom still fresh. Zuhair's skill at unravelling red tape still took hours, but eventually, Margaret said with a smile, "my husband, being a respected professor, worked it out and they got Mam's passport stamped."

The relief they all felt, after waiting for three or fours hours while Zuhair cajoled passport control into letting Olive go, evaporated as they moved through to the next phase: security. Their hearts sank as they watched people up ahead being told to get out of their cars, unload all their luggage and stand passively by while everything was searched, in full view of everyone else in the queue; in some cases the car was pulled apart, too. Margaret got out of their car and, without thinking, walked towards the young American soldiers who were supervising the searches. She didn't realize it at the time, she said, "but they would have been frightened when I approached them that I was setting them up for a car bombing or something." She started to talk. She told them she was British, she showed them her passport, and she told them Olive's story. Her mother was old and frail, she said, and desperately needed medical care that she could get only in Amman. She didn't know, she said, whether her mother could cope much longer with this ordeal. "I really laid it on," Margaret said, laughing. The soldiers listened, their sympathy deepened, and they followed Margaret back to the car to meet Olive. They said hello, talked with her as if she was their own grandmother – asked about her health, how she was holding up, apologized for what she'd been through. And then waved them through the border into Jordan. And they were free.

"I was emotionally exhausted, but it was such an enormous relief to get to the end. When you're leaving Iraq, you can't even tell yourself that you're going somewhere until you make it out and you are safe, and your safety is real. It's only when you cross the border, and you're in Jordan, that you know that you are out. Because you don't know if you will make it or not," Margaret said.

"It was a horrible, emotional time. Just awful. I arrived with two suitcases, and thirty years later, I left with two suitcases."

I I

The View from a Mosul Window

Pauline placed a palm on the large pane of smoked glass overlooking the small stone terrace and out on to her once neat and leafy garden. Silent vibrations tickled her hand. Then the air around her began to hum. She looked out beyond the trees, which for more than twenty years had shaded family barbecues, and squinted into the glare of the overcast sky. As thunder follows lightning, she knew, the cause of her home's sudden fit of the shakes would soon roar into view.

The hum grew in intensity and milky tea began spilling over the sides of the cup that sat on a doily-topped table beside her. Pauline glanced down at it, then up again in time to see a convoy of Bradley Fighting Vehicles – relatively small and lightweight tanks with turrets and treads that carry half a dozen fully armed soldiers – rumble menacingly around the corner. She rolled her eyes as they ripped through the generator cables criss-crossing the street to connect each house to the neighbourhood electricity source. The generator was a cooperative effort, making up for the city grid that provided just a few hours of power a day. The Bradleys lurched to a stop outside her gate and American soldiers jumped down to the street and began cussing at the boys who ran out from the school opposite to demand chocolate. Pauline's doorbell rang. Oh God, they're coming here, she thought, and ran down the stairs to let them in. The front gate crashed in to meet her. "What do you think you're doing?" she shouted at the stunned Americans, clad from head to heel in sand-coloured armour. "Why couldn't you wait for me to open the door? Look what you've done. I was on my way."

"They came to watch the school," recalled Pauline. The junior college opposite her house had regularly been taken over by competing forces within the city. During elections the school was a designated polling booth and had been occupied by Islamists intent on forcing the outcome of the vote in their favour. At various times, Kurdish policemen had taken up positions on the school's roof during campaigns to rid the city of criminals and zealot gangs.

"They came in without a woman, which they're supposed to have with them because during the day the local women are at home by themselves, or just with their children, and the men are out working," Pauline said of the troops. "They were kicking the gate, and I ran down to open it and I told them there was no need for that, I would have opened the door. I told them that's why people are so hostile to you. He was breaking the lock with the butt of his rifle. He said he was very sorry, when he realized I was English-speaking. He said he was just doing what he was told. I said that may be so, but I didn't like it and other people didn't like it.

"The women here are not used to being in the presence of men who aren't members of their families, and when you have these men, in uniform and carrying guns, just barging through your gate and into your house, and after all the things you hear about them on the news, you don't know what they want and can't understand a word they say, it's terrifying. People hate it, and hate them, and that's where the trouble starts. I don't know what they expect, especially when they come by without women soldiers with them. They're tense, too, I understand that. But they don't make friends by breaking doors off hinges.

"All they wanted to do was go on the roof to try and pinpoint sniper fire. I didn't mind. They're very polite, but I don't like them bashing the door down. They want to get in quickly because they're frightened someone's going to take a potshot at them if they stay on the street for longer than a minute or two. This young man, who broke the lock, said: 'We have to get in quick because we don't want anyone taking a shot at us.' I made them coffee and told them they had enough problems without making people dislike them more."

Though Pauline was accepting of their presence, she disapproved of their methods, and couldn't help thinking the men in uniform from her own country would have handled themselves – and the city – much better. "I think the British are better in Basra. From their experience in Northern Ireland, they have better street patrolling and communication. The Americans can be very aggressive. They were effing and blinding at these kids from the school – they were horrible kids, so I could see why. The kids didn't know what they were saying. But we knew. The language was appalling; they were really giving them a mouthful. The kids go running after the tanks because the soldiers used to throw chocolates and sweets. But they don't any more because they don't want anyone near them. If you go near the tanks, they shoot you. They don't even shoot in the air any more. And they don't stop. They totalled a friend's car. Thank goodness he wasn't inside it at the time. They just came roaring around a corner and his car was there and they went right over it in one of these huge Bradley tanks. They go through the generator lines and it costs a lot of money to put them back up, and if one goes, they all go. You understand that they don't want to stop, they're so frightened. But on the other hand, you swear a little bit as well because it costs a lot to repair things."

As insider and outsider, Pauline is able to see both sides of what rapidly became an intractable struggle to gain control of Iraq's present and future. The young men and women of the American armed forces had been told they were coming to Iraq to help rid the country of an evil dictator – a tyrant who, senior members of the US administration insisted, not only had biological, chemical and nuclear weapons of mass destruction but had been collusive with Osama bin Laden in the September 11 attacks that had killed more than three thousand Americans on home soil. Believing this to be their motivation, the foot soldiers of the United States, at the head of their coalition partners, fought to bring freedom, democracy, human rights and the American way of life to a people they had been told would welcome them with rose petals and songs of rejoicing. A quick assault, which wouldn't need too many boots on the ground because the new style of war relied on control of the skies and precision bombing, and Saddam would be gone. Then the grateful Iraqi people would organize an election, vote for a friendly government and get on with rebuilding their country as a shining example of how the Middle East can be remade in the image of a strong, stable, modern, sectarian state.

The self-preservation tactics on display in Pauline's street that day in early 2006 were the inevitable result of almost three years of intensifying insurgency. The reaction of the Americans to constant attacks had only helped deepen disillusionment among Iraqis. The insurgency became more organized – developing from sporadic shootings and grenade firings in the early months after major combat ended, through minor skirmishes, to coordinated military forays in which bands of fighters took control of entire cities. The attacks became more frequent and deadly, and the Americans became even more heavy handed, using sweeping tactics often based on intelligence that was flimsy or just wrong, turning more people against them and strengthening the numbers and support of the insurgency. The only possible result was, as emerged, a vicious circle in which the US soldiers, many of them in their late teens and early twenties, went from chocolate-throwing heroes to frightened devils who shot anyone who came within 50 feet of their tanks and ploughed over cars without even checking whether there was anyone inside. Iraqis who had initially welcomed, albeit cautiously, relief from Saddam's brutality had watched their lives disintegrate and their hopes drain away as their worst fears – that personal, political, ethnic and sectarian revenge and retribution would become the credo of post-Saddam Iraq – became fact. And as long as the incompetent Americans remained, they would be blamed for the hatred that Iraqis unleashed on themselves and on each other.

"They don't like being here," Pauline said, as she related the conversations she'd had with some of the young American men with whom she came into contact as she sat at her window, worrying what the next minutes, hours, days, weeks held for her and her family. She found the soldiers scared, exhausted, confused and angry. They didn't know why they were in a country that they had expected to welcome them unconditionally. But where, it seemed, everyone hated them and wanted them dead.

"There was one, he was nineteen, from Houston, Texas, who had just come back before Christmas. He said: 'I just don't know how I got into all this mess.' I felt so sorry for him. I told him to keep himself safe. He said: 'I'll try.'"

By March, 2006, Pauline had hardly been outside her house for almost a year. She no longer felt secure doing any of the things that make life conventional – walking to the corner kiosk for a loaf of bread; driving into town for her regular weekly afternoon of shopping and tea with Noor; tending the orange trees that now sagged over her wall and dropped their fruit on the footpath below; hanging the family washing on the line stretched across what had been a clipped grass lawn but which had succumbed to weeds. Her house, she felt, was falling down around her because she was too afraid to invite in repairmen. And Ali had even banned her from taking down the curtains to be washed, fearful that without the flimsy layer of privacy they provided, anyone would be able to see in through the huge windows that they had long been so proud of, and spy a household of hated foreigners, bait for extortion, ransom and murder, enemy spies to be made an example of, wrapped in chains and forced to wear orange jumpsuits, the macabre costume of their final moments when their heads would be jerked back by the hair and hacked off from the neck while they screamed in anguish and agony for a worldwide television and Internet audience of billions.

More than most in Mosul, Pauline was a prisoner in her home, with only the fear of what awaited her outside the front gate preventing a descent into stir-crazy, claustrophobic depression. The sole comfort she could derive from her isolation was the knowledge that she was safer sequestered indoors. The fact that she is not Iraqi made her more vulnerable even than her local friends and neighbours to the insanity that had overtaken the city. By now, foreigners had become prime targets, first for criminal gangs – who were also targeting well-to-do Iraqis – just interested in easy money, assuming Westerners had access to stockpiles of cash. And then for zealots such as the psychopathic coward Abu Musab al-Zaqawi – as a Jordanian, also a foreigner – who sought to portray

Westerners as representative of the occupying forces and use their videotaped pleas for mercy, before he cold-bloodedly decapitated them, to force the withdrawal of the foreign troops and turn Western public opinion against their presence in Iraq.

In early March, 2004, the BBC reported that more than 120 foreigners had been taken hostage in Iraq since the invasion and occupation of the country a year earlier. Some had been released amid well-founded suspicions that their governments had negotiated and paid handsome ransoms for their freedom. This inevitably fuelled a grizzly human trade as gangs sprung up simply to kidnap foreigners – often working on tip-offs from the victims' local associates, who were paid for their betrayal – and sell them on to the highest bidder. Eventually, the phenomenon caught the imagination of the Islamist cliques, which saw an opportunity to enhance their own reputations as the hard men of the religious revolution they had come to Iraq to fuel. The American Nicholas Berg was not the first Westerner to be murdered by his kidnappers – that tragic distinction belongs to the Italian security guard, Fabrizio Quattrocchi, who was forced to dig his own grave before being shot, in April, 2003, from behind. A month later, Berg, who at 26 had gone to Iraq in the hope of finding business for his telecoms company, was beheaded on a video that was shown on a regional television network and posted on the World Wide Web. He was the first Westerner to be treated with the savagery that became the trademark of the religious gangs that thus raised the bar of brutality for subsequent kidnappings and murders, whether for profit or for propaganda.

Pauline is acutely aware that the tragedy of Margaret Hassan could have been her own. The trajectories of their lives were so similar as to be parallel. Indeed, if Margaret Hassan had had children of her own, or had Pauline not had children, perhaps each would have followed the other's path.

Margaret Hassan met her husband, Tahseen Ali Hassan, while he was studying in Britain in the early 1960s, and in 1971 they went together to Baghdad. As all foreigners who wanted to remain in Saddam's Iraq were required to, Mrs Hassan became an Iraqi citizen. She worked at the British

Council, the embassy's cultural wing, starting as an English teacher and eventually becoming director before the British pulled their diplomatic presence after the first Gulf War in 1991. Then she joined the Baghdad operation of the charity Care International and worked to counteract the impact of the sanctions that reduced Iraq from a wealthy, developing nation to a country of hungry, ill and dying children. She was well known, respected and liked. She spoke to the British parliament before the 2003 invasion about Iraq's deterioration in the years since the first Gulf War and her belief that another war would be folly.

On October 19, 2004, as she was on her way to work at the Baghdad office of Care, her car was stopped by a group of men wearing police uniforms who pulled her driver from the vehicle and beat him up. When she intervened, Mrs Hassan was taken away. She was seen again only in a number of videos that were released through the same TV network, which has links to terrorist organizations. The videos showed her begging for her life; crying and passing out; having a bucket of water thrown over her; pleading with the British government to withdraw its troops from Iraq. The video of her murder – execution-style with a bullet to the back of the head – was not broadcast, the network bosses saying they "respected the feelings of the audience." (This is difficult to understand. The certainly more gruesome murders of other foreigners – among them the young American telecoms guy, Nick Berg, Briton Ken Bigley, a dozen nameless Nepalese, a handful of Turks – all shown screaming as their heads were being slowly severed – have never inspired this "respect" for the sensibilities of viewers, let alone for the victims and their families.) Six months after Mrs Hassan was murdered, five men admitted to kidnapping and killing her; in mid-2006 three were put on trial; two were acquitted and one was sentenced to life. Mrs Hassan's family blamed the British government for her death and, after the corpse of a Western woman found in Fallujah by American soldiers turned out not to be hers, continue to appeal for the return of her body.

Margaret Hassan's kidnap and murder struck a particular chord with Pauline: "I was always frightened from this thing happening, that they'd take a foreigner married to an Iraqi," she said, "so when we went to town we were careful, we didn't get in taxis or take any risks." She was in Lancashire with Noor, awaiting baby Hussein's arrival, when Mrs Hassan's fate became news. "Someone asked me did I think that they would let her go, and I said no, I think they will kill her because she was working with foreigners, and because she was a foreigner, married to an Iraqi." Those three factors combined made Margaret Hassan the perfect victim, Pauline said – her murderers had a foreigner who was also an Iraqi, who worked for foreigners, whose death would bring pain to Iraqis. "It was upsetting at the time," Pauline said. "When I came back to Iraq, it was frightening."

Pauline says she noticed a very real escalation in the violence after April, 2004, following the murder of four American civilians in Fallujah. Their bodies were mutilated and dragged through the streets in what became irrefutable affirmation that not only were there pockets of resistance to the presence of the American and coalition armed forces – which the governments in Washington and London were trying to downplay – but there was genuine and growing anger among the Iraqi people, too, about the destruction the war had brought, the havoc that had followed, and the breakdown of law and order that prevailed. Fallujah sits within the "Sunni triangle" that stretches from Baghdad on its eastern point to Ramadi in the west and, to the north, Tikrit, home town of Saddam Hussein's clan, from where he drew most of his closest advisers, ministers and generals. Soon after the fall of Saddam's regime, this area became a bastion of resistance to the occupation, and then of inter-sectarian fighting, especially after the bombing in early 2006 of the al-Askirya mosque, in Samarra. The destruction of the shrine, an important one for Shia Muslims, was the signal for Iraq's rupture into civil war.

"That was the start of things, in Fallujah," Pauline said of the attacks on the American contractors – which led to the revenge assault on the city by the Americans and, naturally, a spiralling descent into widespread resentment of the US presence. "From then on, it started to get worse and worse and worse." The shocking way the Americans had been treated – their corpses pulled from a burning vehicle, hacked to pieces, dragged behind a car and hung from a bridge over the Euphrates – not only awoke many in the West to just how big a mess Iraq now was, but rendered life so much more dangerous for the foreigners who had made their home in Iraq and who, like Pauline Basheer and Margaret al-Sharook, were almost indistinguishable from the Iraqis around them.

With this in mind, and an innate awareness that simply being a Westerner made her quarry for criminals and fanatics alike, Pauline and her two children set off in a taxi to Baghdad in early April to collect their British passports from the embassy inside the fortified Green Zone, the hermetically sealed diplomatic and government enclave in the capital. Noor had married seven months earlier, was now pregnant with her first child and planned to have the baby in England. Pauline wanted to take both her children to Britain and hoped that they would choose to stay. In the event, Jamal became ill and couldn't make the journey, and Noor found it difficult to adjust to life in Lancashire and chose to return to Mosul. For the time being, however, the prospect of getting her children out of the Iraqi war zone to the safety of her homeland inspired Pauline to repress her own fear and they took to the road for a nerve-shattering drive to Baghdad and back.

By this time, the stretches of open road between cities had been transformed into a post-apocalypse landscape of vigilantism. Pick-up trucks with machine guns mounted on the cabins, manned by hoodlums with tribal scarves tied around their heads and cocked rocket-propelled grenades strapped across their backs, barrelled across the barren, stony plains, marauding and looting, terrorizing villages, shooting at other vehicles. The roadsides were littered with the detritus of war – overturned rocket-launchers, burned-out tanks, spent shells. Every few miles, massive caches of weapons and ammunition, quite possibly dumped with the purpose of arming the post-war insurgency that Saddam had evidently planned for, sat in open view for the taking. In the tiny clusters of houses that pockmarked the hardscrabble farmland, people hunkered down in trepidation and shot at vehicles they didn't recognize, often rightly fearing that thugs posing as friendly militia come to restore order were vengeful Kurds bent on reclaiming territory they believed was theirs, or looters helping themselves to the spoils.

It was through this Mad Max dystopia that Pauline and her children made the terrible taxi journey to Baghdad for a task as mundane as collecting their passports. Even when the taxi driver, an old friend, paused in Baiji for tea – a regular stop on the road south to the capital for a café where the food is good and where drivers can congregate into convoys they think are safer for the journey – Pauline stayed in the car, and made her children stay with her.

"I was too scared to get out of the car because I didn't want people to see me. Margaret always said that I could pass for Iraqi better than her – my skin is more sallow, she is very white. But people can tell. While we were sitting in the car, another car pulled up and a man got out and just kept walking around our car, and looking at it and in through the windows at us the whole time. I was really, really worried. When the driver came out of the restaurant, I told him about it and he said it's nothing to worry about. We went on and then stopped to get petrol, and this damned car stopped behind us. We were all of us frightened by this stage.

"Then on the way back, we'd just come north of Tikrit near Baiji and there was a car behind us that suddenly veered off the road and over the strip to the other side and rammed into a convoy of American military trucks that were heading in the opposite direction. It didn't explode, so it probably wasn't a car bomb, but there was a huge fire and the radio reported it.

"When we got back, I was glad we got back," Pauline said.

Not long after we got back from the trip to Baghdad, one of Noor's in-laws' relatives was kidnapped from his front door with no warning. He was just fourteen, grabbed off the front step and pulled over the gate. He has never been the same since.

His mother and father were out, with their two eldest daughters. He was at home with a younger brother and sister. They were all inside, doing their homework, and a man who worked for the family, to do the garden and general handyman work, was there with them. The electricity had gone off, and the generator hadn't yet come on, so the lad went outside with the handyman to give it a kick-start. They had to go out into the garden and around the back of the house. While they were out there, the bell at the gate rang, so the lad said to the handyman, you keep working on the generator and I'll go and see who that is.

It was early evening, and already dark, so he couldn't see who was there until he opened the gate. When he did, he saw about twenty men, who had driven up in three cars, and who all started shouting at him. He slammed the gate and tried to run, but one of the men leaned over the gate and grabbed him, dragging him over it. The only sign left of him was his slippers. He was pulled out of his slippers, over the gate and into a car.

He knew what was going on as soon as he saw this huge group of men that he didn't recognize standing outside his gate because gangs had already begun kidnapping children from their schools, targeting the good schools, believing that the parents must have money.

The men bundled the boy into a car and sped off. The other two children came rushing outside to see what was going on. They had heard all the noise and the shouting. The atmosphere in Mosul was very tense at that time, and even the children were frightened of what could happen to them. Parents were telling their children all the time to be careful, to stay indoors, to come straight home from school. Some were sending their children to school with bodyguards. So when the young ones, who were about eight and ten, heard the commotion outside, they rushed out to see what was going on. All they found was his slippers, lying on the path inside the gate, as if he were still standing in them. They immediately knew what had happened. They called their parents and said they thought that Rashid had just been kidnapped. There was no note, no warning and, for two days, no phone call.

When the call did come, it was just to say that they had him, no demands, no information, nothing. But a cousin traced the call to a computer shop in Mosul. At that time, mobile phones had only just been introduced and not everyone had them yet. So to make the call, one member of the gang had to go to a computer shop in town. The caller had said that he would call again at a designated time a couple of days later and that the family were to be waiting to hear from him. So at the said time, the cousin went to the computer shop in town to wait to see who came in. Well, the gang must have recognized him, because they were furious, and told him that if he did it again, or tried to track them down in any way, they'd never see their son alive again.

They asked for $30,000, I think – I didn't ask because it's not something you really talk about, how much ransom you've paid to get your son back alive. It took about a week, seven or eight days, because there were negotiations, and the family was trying to knock down the price. The gangs always ask for ridiculous sums of money because they think that if you're a doctor or a lawyer or professional of some sort, you have lots of money. They don't think that most times the wives aren't working, that it's only one income, and that people just don't have a lot of money that they can put their hands on. They have their homes, and their cars, and usually that's it. When you have gangs asking for tens of thousands of dollars in cash, or they'll kill your son or your father, or your brother or your husband, what can you do? You have to tell them you don't have that sort of money. Then they'll ask, how much do you have, and you have to hope that whatever amount you can raise will be enough.

I talked with the lad, and he told me that he was held in a room in a house in a village outside Mosul. He knew where it was because he knew the direction that they had driven in when they kidnapped him. He said it wasn't dark, and he wasn't blindfolded, that they fed him very well. They didn't smack him, they were rough speaking but they didn't smack him about.

He didn't panic. Even at age fourteen, he didn't cry. He said: "I'd never let them see me cry. I didn't even talk with them unless they talked to me." They looked after him very well. He was one of the first to be kidnapped like that, and at that stage I think it was the criminal gangs, doing it for money. The torture and the beatings and the killings came later.

After their son was kidnapped, no one in the family went out. The older girls stopped going to school and college. One day, while they were all at home, the house was shot up; men drove up and fired on the house while they were all sitting inside. All the windows were shot up, the place was a mess. They could have been killed. That happened three or four times – until the police finally took action and did catch the people who were responsible.

Then, in May [2006], they were threatened again. A note came under their gate, and under every gate on the street. They just ignored it. A friend of mine who is a pharmacist who lives on that street was also threatened – she sent her two sons to Syria to keep them safe. At that stage, it had gone beyond the criminals, and this is how money was being raised to fund the insurgency. They demanded huge amounts of money, and took what they could get. And once they'd spent it, they came back for more. Once you pay, they never leave you alone, it never stops, you're always a target.

The boy had a lot of psychological trauma. He doesn't go to school any more; he was in his fourth year at secondary school, and he just stopped going because he was so frightened. He was terribly traumatized. He couldn't go to the gate, not even out into the garden, he was so frightened. He's still like that. Such a shame. Such a waste.

Noor married into a well-off family of Arab Moslawis, professional people with fingers in many pies. Her father-in-law, Ahmed, had a successful second-hand car dealership; her mother-in-law, Nuha, had trained as a laboratory technician and ran her own successful diagnostic lab. Noor's husband, Mahmood, had a couple of small, thriving businesses of his own, including a boutique stocked with women's clothing from Syria, Jordan and Turkey; and a paper products packaging plant. Noor's in-laws liked to go out, and when they did they promenaded in fine fashion and expensive jewellery. When war came to Mosul in 2003, the family made little effort to modify their habits. They ignored the concerns of neighbours and subtle hints from friends to tone down their flashy behaviour. As safety evaporated, Noor's in-laws carried on with pretty much the same gusto they always had. It came as a surprise to Pauline that Nuha decided to host

Noor and Mahmood's wedding reception at home, rather than in a public hall, because they didn't want to attract too much attention. Nevertheless, it was quite an affair, with a couple of hundred guests, a noisy band and dancing into the wee hours.

In early 2006, Ahmed was kidnapped by an armed gang that stormed his local mosque after Friday prayers, bundled him into a car, tied his hands behind his back with plastic wire, beat him up, ripped his clothes, and dumped him in a septic tank. A demand for $50,000 was sent to his family. They were told that unless they paid, Ahmed would die.

A quietly religious man, Ahmed had prayed at his local mosque five times a day for decades. It was in late January, as he and the hundreds of other worshippers – it was a large and popular mosque – were filing out of the paved courtyard, that three or four cars pulled up, and armed gunmen leapt out and began pushing their way through the crowd. They called out for Ahmed to show himself. The other worshippers, many of whom Ahmed had known all his life, shrank back to let the gunmen through. Only one man stood his ground – the slight, elderly, bearded imam whose voice cut across the cowered crowd as he told the gang to leave this house of God in peace. He was pushed to the ground. Ahmed, struggling and shouting for help, was shoved into one of the cars, and the kidnappers' convoy sped away.

Ahmed shivered in the sewage tank – where he stood literally up to his neck in it – for two days, unable to think through the certainty that he was about to die. Desperate and weak, and not knowing what made him do it, he pushed upwards against the lid. To his astonishment, it lifted. Perhaps not wanting to draw too much attention to their hostage holding pen, the kidnappers had not secured the corrugated iron cover on the tank. Equally astonishingly, nor had they removed the ladder that leaned against the side of the tank. Ahmed, feeble as he was, managed to lift himself over the lip of the tank and climb 12 feet down the ladder. Free, he gathered his thoughts, got his bearings and made his way to the home of a relative not far away. From there he contacted the hysterical Nuha, who along with Mahmood had been trying to raise the cash they'd been ordered to drop off at a designated spot outside Mosul.

Mahmood had already got his hands on an arsenal of firearms, including a machine gun, and found a proxy to deliver the cash to ensure that he himself wasn't also grabbed as he dropped it off on the lonely stretch of road the kidnappers had nominated. When his father called to say he had escaped his captors, the family was overwhelmed with relief. Ahmed then stayed with some relatives on the outskirts of Mosul for a few weeks while he recovered from his ordeal. He knew now that things would have to change. The cars he'd had parked outside his house as part of the business would have to go. No more fancy clothes; restaurants were out; so were parties and large family gatherings. His wife would have to tone down her taste in fashion and jewellery, too.

While Ahmed stayed with his cousins, police drained the tank he'd been held in and found a skull – an earlier victim, they assumed. When Ahmed finally did go home, his kidnappers telephoned incessantly to demand money. Pay up, they warned, or next time you won't be so lucky. "They still pay," Pauline says, "and will have to go on paying. Once you've paid, you have to keep paying."

Eventually, once Ahmed was home, a delegation from the local mosque came to visit, to check on his welfare, they said, and make sure there were no hard feelings. Ahmed saw them off his property. He no longer goes to mosque five times a day; he has long since determined the *qibla* (the direction of Mecca) and so stays home to say his prayers alone. Only on Fridays does he go to mosque, and then to a different one each week, always chosen for its proximity to the home of a relative. After prayers he drops in for lunch, thus rounding out the only trip he will take outside his home until the following week.

The seeds of anarchy, chaos and terror were sown early in Iraq's most recent era of war and occupation, scattered with little regard for the subsequent bitter harvest. If there was any understanding among the American bureaucrats of the consequences their policies would reap for the country and the people they were acting for, then they are largely to blame for the monstrous imbroglio that has ensued.

The best that can be hoped of them is that they acted not with malice aforethought but in ignorance – though the likelihood that this is the case shrinks in direct proportion to the rising mountain of evidence to the contrary. Their culpability will not be diminished either way, but perhaps the Iraqi people, such as the families and friends of Pauline and Margaret, who have suffered inordinately as a direct consequence, will be able to understand how those people whose actions have blighted the lives of so many can sleep at night.

"The governments in the West, in London and Washington, thought it would be just like Desert Storm [the First Gulf War of 1991], quick and easy and all over in no time," Pauline said as she looked back on how the debacle developed. "Everyone in Iraq knew that it would end up like this, with people coming from abroad to exploit the chaos, and people here fighting each other. We all knew it would be civil war because they just can't get on with each other – Sunnis and Shias don't get on, Arabs and Kurds don't like each other, the Turkomen don't like the Arabs. There is a lot of resentment – he [Saddam] took land off one group and gave it to another and gave nothing in return; it's created a lot of resentment.

"Everyone here could see it," she continued. "Those who wanted to come back from overseas and become the new government couldn't see it because they didn't understand the nature of the people, they'd been gone for so long and didn't know what Saddam had made of the people here, how they hated him, hated each other, hated themselves. The governments in America and Britain couldn't see it because they had no idea either; they just listened to the exiles. It was people who didn't know taking advice from people who didn't know. But the people in Iraq knew what would happen – and that's exactly what did happen."

Like many of the politicians, academics, journalists, writers and analysts who have attempted to understand what went wrong in Iraq after the invasion and occupation of 2003, Pauline believes that the decision by the head of the occupying authority, Paul Bremer, to dismantle the civil service, along with the police and military, was the single major mistake of the occupation, a milestone in the making of the Mesopotamian morass.

Paul Bremer arrived in Baghdad in early May, 2003, to take the place of Lieutenant General Jay Garner, whose early stewardship of the occupation had been deemed ineffectual and incompetent. Garner had arrived with little idea of what to expect once the major conflict ended and little evident understanding of the internecine communal battles that were bubbling under. But he did at least move slowly and try to make contact with senior community leaders. His graceless departure was the first indication that Washington didn't know what it was doing. Events that followed confirmed the encroaching dread.

Almost before Bremer had even changed out of his Washington brogues and into the tan desert boots that he wore as a trademark throughout his tenure as head of the Coalition Provisional Authority, as the quasi-colonial administration was called, he took three pivotal steps: he dissolved the Iraqi army; he sacked all members of the Ba'ath Party of a certain rank and above from their civil service jobs; and he curtailed moves towards the creation of an interim domestic government. On May 16, five days after landing in Baghdad and without any apparent attempt at wide-ranging consultation on what impact such sweeping moves might have on the social landscape, Bremer transformed Iraqis from friends-in-waiting to resentful foes. Suddenly, hundreds of thousands of people were without work and income, caught in the net of Bremer's De-Ba'athification Order, which appeared to have been issued without regard for the possibility that membership of the Ba'ath Party was often a condition for getting, holding and being promoted in a job. The American journalist and author George Packer, in his book *The Assassins' Gate*, quotes a Kirkuk father of nine who had worked as a safety officer at an oil company for 32 years and had been a member of the Ba'ath Party for 28 years before Bremer sacked him. "Every country has its system," he said. "In Iraq it was the Ba'ath Party." Waddah Ali, a poet and university lecturer who worked with the American military as a translator after the invasion and now lives in exile, said: "Under Saddam Hussein, if you were not a member of the Ba'ath Party, you wouldn't get rations, you'd be forbidden to study, you wouldn't be on the earth but in the sea." By de-Ba'athing Iraq, Bremer served neither Iraqi nor American interests, but fuelled those of terror and insurgency.

In Mosul, the ramifications of these knee-jerk decisions were devastating. The city was one of Saddam's major military zones, a recruiting centre for the armed forces, and home to many senior military leaders who had long political and social tentacles – men who should have been nurtured as supporters of the new Iraq, rather than treated as outcasts of the old regime. Now they were surplus to requirements. If Garner's removal had told of Washington's weakness, Bremer's appointment and immediate actions demonstrated what many people interpreted as the American administration's sinister intent – to run their country as a vassal state. Suspicions had flared when, during the looting of Baghdad, the only building protected by American troops was the Oil Ministry. Now nearly everyone was out of a job, hardly anyone was getting paid, civic infrastructure was not being rebuilt, there was no discernible law, and American firms with links to the White House were being handed multi-billion-dollar contracts to rebuild and run the oilfields. All Bremer did was lay mulch for the disillusionment and disarray that had already taken root.

"It wasn't that bad at the start," Pauline says as she remembers the first days and weeks after the fighting ended. "Everyone was, well, they were happy and hoping everything would be OK. I used to go into town to telephone my mum and relatives. Everyone was friendly, the kids gathered around the Americans who parked their vehicles in the streets. It got worse when Bremer sacked all the party people and dismantled everything. So many people were unemployed, and they started to form small groups. And people could see that their worst fears were about to come true."

The worst of it, she believes, is the loss of community spirit. Pauline went from moving freely around her adopted home, to limiting her excursions to essential trips for food and supplies, to, ultimately, locking herself indoors. She and the handful of other foreign wives of Iraqi men who remained in Mosul cut down on their telephone contact in case the lines were bugged and the wrong people would hear them speaking English. Her days were punctuated with the constant phone calls she demanded from Jamal – when he got to college, as he moved from class to class, as he chose a taxi for the short trip home. If he was late calling – often just because the mobile network was jammed or down – she panicked, fearing that their time had come.

"There is nothing in my life. I never do anything or go anywhere. Once or twice I've ventured out. Ali took me out a couple of times. He told me later that he dreaded it and was terrified, but he wanted to give me some pleasure. But he told me that the whole time he was worried that something would happen," Pauline said.

"I did something really daft one day. There was a woman outside the gate with two little children, and one of them picked up an orange that had fallen off our tree. The other one started to cry because he didn't have an orange, so I went down and opened the gate and gave the woman an orange for the child. Ali was furious, said I could have been grabbed by anyone, that it could have been a set-up. She was very nice and very grateful. But it was a stupid thing to do. You can't trust anyone."

Not even those you pray with. Ali's local mosque organized a rubbish collection to make up for the lack of civic hygiene services, but after a few months he thought better of having people he didn't know coming to his house, so he and Jamal began making the trip to the nearest dump twice a week themselves. After Ahmed's ordeal, Ali, also a religious man and a regular attendee of Friday prayers, stopped going to mosque.

"Ahmed is not a scared type, but he is always wary now, locking the gate and the doors and jumping at any noise. He won't go out, and he doesn't go to the same mosque twice. The children might not admit that they are scared, but Thamir often carries guns in his car – he registered them with the Americans after what happened to his father. They'll never admit to being frightened because that amounts to weakness. But I'm terrified. The only thing I'm not afraid of is saying that I'm afraid."

جسر الملك غازي / موصل

12

"We've had some terrible news ..."

Three years to the day after Mosul's fall, Pauline, Ali and Jamal fled the city for their lives.

Three days earlier, on April 8, Ali had answered his phone to a man who said he was with "Islamic Jihad" – a name synonymous with terrorism – demanding $10,000 or Jamal would be kidnapped and killed. "I don't have that sort of money," Ali told him. "I don't have any money. I have my house, my clinic and my car, that's it."

"You'll find the money if we take your son from his college," the caller said. "I know where your house is, I know where your son is." The voice on the end of the phone said Ali was to go to his clinic the next day, Saturday, and await instructions.

Ali didn't tell Pauline about the threat. Instead, he called some of his vast clan, who arrived at his home the following morning in a no-nonsense, gun-toting posse and for the rest of the day enveloped him as an amoeba does its nucleus, determined nothing was going to happen to Ali on their watch. Ali closed his clinic to patients and spent the day locked inside, waiting for the phone call that would decide his family's fate.

The bodyguard was no sham – Ali knows terrorists are cowards at their core. "It's when people are alone," Pauline said as she recalled how one of Ali's colleagues, while out walking alone, had been dragged into a moving car as pedestrians stopped to watch. "Scared for themselves, I suppose," she said of the bystanders with barely concealed disgust.

Ali waited in his clinic as ordered. No call came. Ali was convinced that no contact meant Jamal had already been snatched from outside his college. With no means of paying the ransom, and expecting the worst – that the next time they saw their son, he and Pauline would be weeping over his corpse – Ali collapsed. The stress stabbed him in the chest so severely he thought he was having a heart attack. His protective clansmen drove him home and carried him into the house. "I can't stand it," Ali told Pauline. "We have to leave."

As soon as she saw her husband, weak, ashen faced and barely able to stand, Pauline guessed what was going on. But she said she had no idea which emotions were fiercest as Ali explained to her what he'd been through over the previous 24 hours – the panic, fear and dismay as she realized that the nightmares she'd lived for the past three years had come true; or the simple fury she felt with her husband for having hidden this truth from her. She had been warning Ali for months that their turn for threats, kidnapping, extortion and, probably, flight was getting nearer by the day. "What makes you any different from anyone else?" Pauline asked him whenever he tried to calm her with assurances that they had nothing to worry about. "Relatives have been telling him for three years – you're a doctor, your wife is English, your son is an easy target because he goes out to college every day," Pauline said. "But Ali just couldn't believe he would be a target."

Jamal came back from college that Saturday afternoon to a house chilled by dread. When he heard from his father of the threat that had been hanging over his life, he was violently ill. He spent that night and most of the next day vomiting, sweating and retching as the bile of other people's senseless hatred welled up within him, and his body purged the distilled terror that had swept over him as his father's story unfolded. A timid and sickly young man, Jamal had for a couple of years been taking every precaution his parents forced on him. He caught a taxi to college every day and phoned his mother when he arrived. After each class, he phoned to say he was leaving one lecture and was on his way to another. When his classes finished for the day, he rang to say he was out of school.

Sometimes he would cross the road from his college and browse in the computer, mobile phone and DVD stores opposite. Other days, he would go directly to the nearby taxi rank and, after calling his mother to say he was on his way, he would check out the drivers and choose a car by gut instinct, never really sure he'd get home safely.

Caution had crept into every corner of life in the Basheer household. Beneath Ali's assurances that they would not be targeted was a profound awareness that prudence was their best protection. It had long been clear that Pauline's foreignness was the family's greatest liability. A low profile had become habitual. Pauline rarely left the house, and never alone. When she went with Jamal to shop, they were discreet, buying only essentials. When they came home, they drove into the garage and locked the door before taking anything out of the car. Pauline began wearing headscarves so as not to draw attention to herself. Ali had stopped going to mosque. Repairs to the house went undone, as Ali did not want contractors coming in and seeing his English wife and half-English son and concluding they were the makings of a lucrative kidnap plot. In this atmosphere, no one in Mosul who was not a relative could be trusted. And perhaps not even then.

Theories flew about who was behind the threats to the Basheers. Many in Ali's extensive family network were convinced they came from a renegade relative who they knew had tried a similar scheme two years earlier. At that time, his targets were the couple who nearly three decades ago had turned up on Ali and Pauline's doorstep while she prepared for one of her first dinner parties as a newly-wed. To her shock, they had taken over her kitchen to cook themselves a meal, and Ali had simply laughed and told Pauline it was just the Iraqi way and she'd get used to it. By 2005, the cousin had become a respected judge in Mosul's nascent post-war judiciary, doing his part to rebuild the legal infrastructure of the shattered city. One evening, a letter arrived under the front gate of his house demanding US$70,000 or his teenage daughter would be taken from her college. The judge didn't bother trying to trace the source of the threat. He, his wife and the three of their seven children still at home piled into the family car and left Mosul for good.

Talk among the extended Basheer family only added to Ali and

Pauline's confusion, chagrin and discombobulation. By this stage, it seemed as if most of the people they knew had been, at the very least, threatened. Lives were being ruined all around them. Pauline and Ali spent intense days and nights analysing every move and word of everyone they had come into contact with for weeks, trying to glean tiny clues as to who on earth was shattering their world.

Many people received notes, but they had received none. The voice of the kidnap caller was of a young man who spoke standard Arabic – so not a Kurd, then. And not, by his accent, a native of Mosul. Where could he have come from? Did he work alone? If not, was he a gangster, or was he a jihadi? Was he, perhaps, a student at the university who had taken offence at something Ali had done or said? Had he failed an exam that Ali had supervised or marked and this was his revenge? Ali remembered that one of the tail-lights of his car had been smashed – had someone kicked it in as a warning he'd not heeded? They picked over half-remembered incidents – an unrecognized man who had walked past the house once, or maybe twice; the phone had rung a couple of times one day, but stopped before Pauline could answer it. Hadn't one of the guards at Jamal's college looked at him a little strangely the other week? And why was the hospital gateman asking so many questions lately? It all turned and churned in Pauline's mind, until each snippet took on the gargantuan proportions of an omen they should have spotted, a hint of danger they had foolishly ignored, the point on which their lives were now pivoting. Her questions – which all boiled down to who? and why? – went frustratingly, maddeningly unanswered.

Pauline telephoned Noor to tell her what was going on. Mahmood was at the door within the hour to deliver a machine gun and a revolver that he insisted Pauline and Ali learn how to use. "Don't ask me where he got them, but he has a licence for them and the Americans allow him to have them because of what happened to Ahmed," Pauline said. "Can you imagine? Ali with a machine gun and me with a revolver?"

They spent the next 24 hours packing up the house. Panicked and sleepless, they barricaded themselves inside. On the morning of Monday, April 11, 2006, as soon as morning prayers were finished and Mosul's famous bridges had reopened with the end of curfew, Pauline, Ali and Jamal piled themselves and a meagre selection of their belongings into their wheezing old Mazda and drove to safety in Dohuk, 25 miles and a universe away in the Kurdish mountains.

"I arrived with two suitcases," Pauline said, in an unconscious echo of Margaret's words, of the day 26 years earlier when she and Ali had pulled up at his mother's house in Mosul to embark on their new life together. "And I left with two suitcases."

13

Life Begins Anew

The setting sun glowering through Pauline's kitchen window raises the temperature in the room to well above the 46 degrees Celsius (115 Fahrenheit) it is outside. The electricity from the local grid went off hours ago, and the man who came to fix the generator had to go for more parts; he probably won't be back for days. The water in the electric cooler is warm by now, the frozen ceiling fan mere decoration. Pauline and I move the glass-topped dining table out of the line of the sun blazing in through the open door. She sits down, perspiration dampening her grey-streaked hair, which is pulled softly back by a butterfly clip, and begins to stuff the dolma she is making for dinner. My eyes are stinging and watering from the toxic mixture of concrete dust and petrochemical fumes that taints the sun an unnatural orange as it droops lower in what feels like an interminable trajectory towards darkness.

Pauline chats – and in this energy-sapping, brain-deadening heat it is hard to know how she can function at all – as she scoops the filling she has made of rice and tinned tomatoes and minced lamb into the hollowed-out gourds of eggplant and squash, rolls it into onions and spinach leaves, and carefully places each dolma into a large pot that has a couple of thick lamb chops in the bottom. On her six-burner stove she's got stock boiling, and some chicken. And in the oven she's heating a large kibbeh, a traditional Mosul meat pie made with cracked-wheat pastry. Now and then she takes a tissue and dabs at the perspiration glistening on her forehead and neck.

The previous evening, she recalled, there had been a breeze, so they'd all dragged their mattresses on to the tiled terrace outside the kitchen door and slept beneath the stars until the flies began to bite at around 5 a.m. "You can't do that any more in Mosul," she said. "It was just what you did, all the time. But now nobody does. It's too dangerous, with bullets flying around. You don't know when something is going to start up, firing and bombing. So you stay indoors. And if there's no electricity, and it's too hot to sleep, you just don't sleep."

In Dohuk things are different. There is peace here. It is not fragile, but it is vulnerable. Turkey's government is threatening to send troops over the border to quell Kurdish PKK rebels it says are still fighting a low-level war of independence and killing around a dozen people a month in its eastern Kurdish region. Iran is shelling the bases of Iranian Kurds inside Iraqi Kurdistan. Like the Turks, Tehran is accusing them of "acts of terrorism" on Iranian soil. In recent weeks in and around Dohuk there have been sporadic arrests of putative suicide bombers, and local security has been tightened amid rumours that Shia militia are infiltrating from the troubled south. Pauline has noticed that, for the first time since she arrived in Iraqi Kurdistan three months ago, the traffic police are now carrying guns, and that more cars are being stopped and searched at the city's major checkpoints. It makes her feel safe. Security here is not arbitrary or partisan. There are none of the blue police uniforms that elsewhere in Iraq have come to be feared rather than trusted. From today, Ali has heard, Arabs are not being allowed into the city unless they have official permission. In Dohuk, as elsewhere in this eastern corner of Iraq, there is zero tolerance for those who resent the peace that Kurds have held hard to over the past decade, and which they have no intention of giving up. Any threat to the status quo is more likely than not to push the Kurds away from their compact with Iraqi federalism and towards the dangerous notion of independence. With war between Lebanon and Israel occupying the headlines, it is possible that Iran and Turkey are taking advantage of the cover that the conflict is providing to inflict a little argy-bargy of their own on the Kurds.

For now, though, the Basheers are focusing on what Dohuk has to offer them. "Look," says Ali, as he drives me back to the Hallal Hotel after our sweltering dinner, "people park their cars on the streets. In Mosul, they would be stolen. In Mosul, people take the wheels off their cars so they will not be stolen; they take the batteries out so they won't be stolen. Here, they do not even lock their cars." Indeed, many people here don't lock their front doors.

Dohuk is a Kurdish boom town. Half an hour's drive through half a dozen checkpoints from Mosul, it may as well be on a different planet. People walk in the streets, wave down taxis, wander through the souk, do their shopping (or simply check the prices) at the big Mazi supermarket built with Turkish money and owned by the local prime minister, and where Pauline comes for Horlicks and Quaker oats, most other things being available cheaper elsewhere. Children play outside; elderly peshmerga sit around drinking chai. Many women wear the black, cover-all abaya; many don't. And on a hill by the Hallal Hotel is a huge, newly built church with a cross etched into its spire. New suburbs are springing up, shops are opening everywhere, and rents on houses, apartments and offices are going through the roof. Autonomous Kurdistan has stable government, a loyal security force, an ardent trickle of investment from abroad, and a determination that the chaos ripping through the rest of Iraq won't encroach on the highest standard of living in the country.

In the three years since I was last here, the city has ballooned, and it seems that in every direction I turn there are new buildings going up, and on some of them the work continues around the clock. Roads and bridges are turning small-town Kurdistan into an important regional centre of trade and business with ambitions to rival Irbil, less than a hundred miles to the south. In the evenings, Dohuk's roads are choked with new cars, from Hondas to Humvees, and on Friday nights it's a race to secure a table in the sprawling garden restaurants along the riverbanks. Dream City amusement park is heaving until past midnight, the lights of its Ferris wheel twirling gaily over the low-rise skyline. The population here has expanded so rapidly since the war that development can hardly keep up. This is a town desperately in need of drainage and garbage collection.

Pauline, who has come from the squalor and stench of Mosul, where civic services broke down three years ago, doesn't notice the rotting rubbish and stagnant water filling the gutters here. "To me, Dohuk is clean," she says. "It's lovely."

Dohuk is easy enough to reach from outside the country, with two airlines flying into Iraqi Kurdistan a few times a week – though what's written on the ticket doesn't always mean what it says. I bought a $500 ticket from Iraqi Airlines to fly from Dubai to the regional capital of Irbil, but landed, corkscrew-style, in Sulaymaniyah and was eventually provided with a taxi for the three-hour journey north-east to Irbil. There, I hired an armoured BMW driven by an armed Christian called Alexander for a two-hour drive to Dohuk, taking one of three possible routes, but the one that went closest, and therefore most treacherously, to Mosul.

It was a familiar journey, and one I'd made numerous times in 2003, when I'd been covering the war as a reporter. Then, I had met Pauline and Margaret by accident and serendipity. This time Pauline was my destination, and she'd been telling me constantly throughout the week before my arrival that she was losing sleep over my safety. Reassured that I was able to take responsibility for myself, and that I was going into a danger zone with both eyes open, she had said: "It's just me, I'm a worrier." But when the plane was diverted to Sulaymaniyah, and the lack of mobile phone contact between one side of Iraqi Kurdistan and the other meant she couldn't track me down, she was captive to Alexander's stories of what might be holding me up – passed on to her via a network of contacts and relatives and so embellished at every telling – which at one stage of the afternoon had me in Baghdad. By the time I finally reached Dohuk, five hours later than expected, Pauline was in such a state I felt forced to apologize to her for all the anguish involved in waiting for me.

For there can be no underestimating the danger of these roads. As I walked around the Dohuk souk one afternoon with Pauline and the son of her friend Hassina, the lad pointed to a half-finished building and said its owner had been kidnapped on the road between Kirkuk and Dohuk, a stretch of highway that after the war in 2003 had reminded me of the nihilistic badlands of the Mad Max movies, controlled by marauding gangs, their faces covered with chequered scarves and their fingers teasing the triggers of machine guns and rocket-propelled grenades.

Today, the roads are still in poor condition; there are signs they are being widened and resurfaced but progress is slow because bitumen, which must come from Baiji or Baghdad, is difficult to obtain. The Kalak bridge that was bombed to dust by the retreating Iraqi army has been repaired, and the war debris of burned-out tanks and dead donkeys is long gone. The roadside petrol-heads are still here, going slowly mad on the fumes of the fuel they're selling. But the 20-mile stretch that passes through the Mosul governorate is twenty minutes of tension that made me grateful for the black screens on the back windows of the BMW and the Glock pistol shoved down beside the handbrake. The three or four checkpoints through what was once no man's land between Saddam's Iraq and the line of control delineating protected Kurdistan are manned by Arabs wearing police uniforms. Here, the uniform means little more than gun for hire, and too often zealots and insurgents have hired that gun. My visit overlapped with the anniversary of the Ba'athist revolution from July 17 to July 30, 1968. The murders, car bombs and suicide attacks were continuing down south; Ba'athist anger was palpable. So I kept my head discreetly behind the driver's seat and hoped the afternoon heat had sucked the "bad guys" dry of any energy for caring that there might be a foreigner in the back seat on her way to Dohuk.

Late one Sunday night in April, Pauline had left a message on my answering service. "Hello, Lynne," said her quavering voice. "We've had some bad news. We've been threatened and we are going to have to leave. I'll be in touch with you soon."

For days I had no way of knowing where she was or tracking her down, so I booked myself on flights to Amman and Damascus, thinking that if the family was leaving Iraq, the first stop would likely be either Jordan or Syria. Then an e-mail arrived:

Sorry to frighten you but it just came too fast. Ali went to the clinic and some animal called him and said they wanted 10 thousand dollars or they would kidnap Jamal from college. Ali told him we didn't have that kind of money. The caller threatened him and told him he would ring again on Saturday. Ali went to the clinic but there was no call. We were living a nightmare. Yesterday we decided to pack up and leave. We made it to Dohuk this morning but Noor is safe with her family.

We left everything, just bringing what we could carry. We are staying with relatives who were also threatened until we find somewhere to live. In the last few days, we are about the twelfth doctor's family to leave and many more are threatened, but have decided to stay. I will sign off now because it is not my computer. I will be in touch as soon as I can.

Over the following few weeks, we spoke almost daily, using the Skype free Internet phone service. Pauline rode an emotional roller coaster, and found little solace in Ali's inability to grasp the reality of their situation. His depression, she said, made her wonder if he would cope over the long term; and if he couldn't cope, she didn't know how she would. What little self-confidence she'd possessed had drained away over the course of the three post-war years she had spent indoors. Now, in a strange place, with little to do and few friends, not knowing her way around and still afraid to venture out of doors alone, Pauline felt isolated and bored. With time on her hands, she dwelled on what had happened to them, and in so doing pushed herself deeper into the depression. Sometimes when we talked she wept with the frustration and rage she felt about having control over her life wrested from her. "We are better off here, it's better than Mosul," she said one day. Then she added: "It doesn't help, though."

She kept in constant touch with Noor; they were missing each other terribly. Noor came to visit a couple of times, and having her and the toddler around seemed to help bring Pauline out of herself. My visit, too, had helped, she said. She'd realized on the day we walked around the Dohuk souk, and she'd insisted on buying me a beautiful and elaborately embroidered crimson jilbab made in Indian Kashmir, that there was no danger in venturing into the centre of town. "I can do that by myself here, people are nice and it's OK to walk around by yourself and without a headscarf. I feel better knowing that," she said.

The most difficult thing to get used to had been the quiet. No bombs, no gunfire, no helicopters. The silence was spooky. "I don't think you ever get over it," said Pauline, evoking her timidity. "Even when I go back to England, I hear a bang and I jump a mile."

The judge, Faoud, and his wife, Hassina, who settled in Dohuk after their flight from Mosul two years earlier, assured her she would, eventually, get used to it. Having been through exactly the same experience, they exude empathy for their cousins' plight. They opened their home to Pauline, Ali and Jamal upon their arrival, and helped them work through their initial shock and upset. Within days, Hassina and her daughters took Pauline on a shopping tour of the city, and she was astounded to see security men without guns, American soldiers parking their Humvees and tanks in the street outside the Mazi and sauntering in, unencumbered by body armour, to buy ice-cold Cokes. Sure enough, as we sit in the café of the Mazi complex, where you can buy anything from barbecues to trail bikes, Pauline points to the family groups sitting at the aluminium tables around us, sipping 7-Up and eating Magnum ice creams. Life here is pretty conventional. "It's another world," Pauline says. "It's hard to imagine that just forty-five minutes' drive away down the road there's Mosul and everything that goes with that."

Faoud called on his contacts to get the necessary documents for Ali to bring in some furniture from the house in Mosul. With his network of relatives in useful positions throughout the local administration, it took less than a week to get done. Then Faoud organized another group of relatives to go around to the Basheer house and pile beds, sofas, the television, Jamal's computers and books and some kitchenware, including the new six-burner stove, on to an open truck to bring through the checkpoints to Dohuk. "They were scared, worried that whoever had made the threats against us could be watching the house and start shooting," Pauline said of the men who went into the house she and Ali had built seventeen years earlier to pick through her belongings and decide what would follow them into enforced exile. "Noor went over to help clean up, and it was very upsetting for her, seeing what was left, and looking at half-empty rooms that she had grown up in. It's all locked up now, and the neighbours are looking after the garden, watering the trees. It seems to be OK, but we've told Noor not to go around there, for her own safety. You don't know if anyone is watching it, waiting for one of us to turn up. The neighbours say everything is OK, but I worry about it because the Americans often blow up houses that stand empty for too long because, sometimes, insurgents move in and use them for bomb factories and then disappear. We have one friend who lived in Baghdad, who moved out of his house after being threatened. The Americans came along and blew it up, destroyed every-thing, they said because someone had told them that insurgents had taken it over. Who knows if that's right? The Americans have been so willing to listen to whatever they're told, it could have just been someone talking so that the house would be blown up. Who knows? You can never know the truth any more."

Ali had already been approached by Dohuk University about taking a senior academic post, and after the threats and the family's hurried departure, the dean of Mosul University said he would be only too willing to help by pushing through a transfer. But first, he said, take six months' sabbatical to see whether the situation changes and you want to come back. With a real estate agent, Ali found a clinic near the Dohuk souk, and within weeks had set up his nameplate. As well as new drop-in business, patients began turning up from Mosul, and others who had feared the trip to Mosul since security went to hell began travelling from all over Iraqi Kurdistan to see him. Everywhere he went, he ran into former patients and their families. Out of nowhere, a man knocked on the door of the newly opened clinic and said that fifteen years earlier Ali had treated his mother. He'd heard about Ali's recent troubles, he said, and wanted to do what he could – so he offered to print all the clinic's stationery at his printing works for free. One morning during my visit to Dohuk in July, 2006, Ali, Pauline and I were chatting in the foyer of the Hallal Hotel before heading out into the blazing summer heat, when the owner of the hotel approached to say that his mother had been a patient of Ali's a few years earlier, and if there was anything he could do for Ali and his family – and friends, he said, gesturing towards me – we only had to ask.

Ali is a great loss, not only to his patients in Mosul, but also to Mosul University. When Ali called the dean to ask about progress on his transfer application, the dean told him he'd lost the paperwork. "You're not coming back?" he asked Ali. "It's sorted out in Mosul." Ali asked him: "Are you still walking around with your two bodyguards and your gun?" The dean admitted that, yes, he was. "Then it's not sorted out in Mosul," Ali said, making it plain he has no plan, at least not for now, to return. The dean promised to get things moving, and within days the transfer was complete and Ali's status in Dohuk formalized.

Jamal decided to turn down an offer from the dean that he stay with his family in Mosul while taking his second-year exams, which were scheduled for a couple of weeks after the kidnap threat against him. Neither Pauline nor Ali wanted him to take the risk of returning to Mosul, and Jamal, who had just turned 21, rather liked the idea of being idle for a few months. "I don't mind, it's a holiday," he said. And it gave him time to decide on how and where he would continue his degree in agricultural studies. So he hangs out, surfs the Internet, indulges his fascination for Japan and Hong Kong, watches DVD movies and plays games on his laptop, helps his parents settle in, and accompanies his mother whenever she leaves the house. He likes Dohuk, he says. What's not to like? It's quiet and safe and peaceful. Though with his mother still preoccupied with his safety on the streets, he has yet to venture out much to meet new friends his own age.

Other relatives of Ali's, living in Sweden, offered their house, newly built on a hill in an area called Hael Melein, which can loosely be translated as Millionaire's Row. Pauline calls it Toy Town as each house is painted a different colour. Hers is avocado green. From her kitchen, Pauline can look out on the rolling Kurdish hills that stretch due north into Turkey and form a backdrop for the multicoloured mansions that stand on the other side of the wide, unmade road. She has a small garden plot that she'll get someone in to plant once spring arrives. "I've lost interest, to tell the truth. You put so much effort into making things nice, and then you lose everything," she said wistfully, thinking of the garden she nurtured in Mosul for seventeen years. She has two large bedrooms, a living room and the "best room," a couple of bathrooms and the huge kitchen. Upstairs is plenty of storage, and downstairs what would have been a double garage has been divided in two with half leased as a shop. It's the done thing now, Pauline said, to rent the ground level as commercial space, especially in Mosul, where people no longer want to leave their neighbourhoods to make the trip into the centre of town. "It's a good income for the owners," she said. "And people feel safer not having to go so far." Rent on the relatives' house is reasonable in a city with an increasingly tight housing market, and they feel fortunate; at $500 a month, it is half what they would otherwise have to pay for the same size and neighbourhood. They've bought an apartment in a complex not far away that is being built by a Turkish developer. They will have paid it off by the time it is finished, in 2008, and that's where they plan to make their home long-term – as long as it is impossible to return to Mosul.

"I hope we can go back to Mosul," Pauline said. "This doesn't feel like home. I know we're lucky and that we have so much, really, but I want to go back to Mosul. I have nothing that makes a life here, I don't know anyone, I have no friends. That's where I have friends, it's where I know and feel at home, and I feel it's all been taken away from me."

Pauline might be aware that in relative terms they have landed on their feet, but that doesn't erase the regrets she has about being forced to leave Mosul. Or the anger she feels at the way in which her life has been changed. "If anyone were to ask me do you want this or do you want him [Saddam] back, I'd say bring him back. At least I could go outside. I didn't have to be afraid of having my head chopped off. You knew where you stood, and what you could and couldn't do. Not any more."

Her views on this are diametrically opposed to those of Ali, whose few pronouncements betray his belief that life under a dictator is the worst sort of miserable existence. Yet when she ponders the past three decades, Pauline concedes that if she had the power to rewrite and relive history, she would erase Saddam from the portrait of her life and give her children what everyone is entitled to: normality.

"I regret it every day," she says as we sit together in my suite at the Hallal Hotel, her reminiscences coming to an end and her thoughts turning to what might have been. "I regret staying here in Iraq, and I regret it more now than I did in Mosul."

In 1985, when the Iran–Iraq War was in full swing, she and Ali and five-year-old Noor went to England to visit her family. Pauline was pregnant with Jamal and planned to give birth to him in the UK. Ali was intending to complete the paperwork so that he could stay and they could resettle as a family in Britain. This was when Ali's elderly mother somehow got wind that he wanted to emigrate, and made him promise to come home, which he did after just a month. "I wouldn't have split us up," Pauline says of her decision to return to Mosul a little later, with the two children. "But I couldn't have imagined that all this" – three decades of war, fear, deprivation, terrorism and, ultimately, death threats – "would have happened."

She sighs, shifts in the big, black, faux leather armchair, passes a hand over her face to push aside a wisp of hair, and takes a sip of water. "I regret it every day that Ali didn't stay when we had the chance. I regret that the kids have never known anything but war. They've never seen much of anything, they missed out on a lot of things. Even just going to England in the summers or at Christmas, which would have been normal. Or going outside to countries nearby like Jordan, or Syria, or Turkey. Iraqi people weren't allowed to travel. And if you're not able to travel, you don't learn about other cultures.

"I don't think they would have turned out to be different from the people they are today if this had been a normal country. It's the same everywhere you go – some people are nice, some people are not nice. The other temptations – drugs, drink, smoking – who knows if they would have got into that," she says, remembering the vortex of addiction and crime that she saw swallow many of the children of Colne, and specifically those of two close friends who ended up in prison. "It doesn't matter what background you come from, drugs can get you, and I believe that if we had been in England, mine could have ended up that way. The irony is that life is better here in a war zone for my kids than for many of the children of people my age in Colne."

On the other hand, she says, "they've never had a life, we've never had a holiday. And so their world view is narrower, and their experiences are so much shallower than they would have been, and I regret that."

And for herself? Is she a different person for the experience of living through the brutality of Saddam's reign, her time in Iraq having tracked his presidency, if not his trajectory of power, from start to finish?

"My mother says I've become hard, but you have to toughen up to survive here. It's every man for himself; it's survival of the fittest. The people have to be hard to get through this sort of life. It's been an eye-opener. Some people have experienced not one war. But three! It makes you a stronger person, you realize that you can adapt to anything to survive. And along the way you learn things about yourself. I think it has made me a better person. You have to be hard, but you have to have compassion, too. If you don't have compassion, you're not really a person, just a lump of stone.

"Your feelings might harden but it's because you have to put up with a lot more than you would in England, where people have so much and take it all so much for granted. It might do a lot of people a lot of good to have the experiences that I have had; they might think about other people more.

"People outside just can't imagine what it has been like – the bombings, the murders, and how people react. Like the time there were four Europeans, electricians, I think, who were killed and their bodies thrown in a ditch by the side of the road. And the cars were just driving past; no one was stopping to even try to help. It makes you wonder what you would do – probably the same, because if you stop to help other people, you can be opening yourself up to danger."

Or the time when a telegram came from home in Lancashire to tell her that her father had died – she didn't get it for two days, even though it had been opened and read at every step of its journey to her, because no one, she says, wanted to be the one to deliver the bad news. "Just imagine that," she says with a resignation born of decades of separation.

❧

By the time my visit is done and I find myself on the next-to-most dangerous road in the region, the workman has turned up with the parts needed to get Pauline's generator working. For the first time in weeks, she and Ali and Jamal have a comfortable night's sleep, and she can prepare dinner admiring the view from her kitchen window rather than resenting the power of the evening sun that exacerbates her lifelong hatred of the heat.

Now her thoughts are turning to other things as Noor's second baby, another boy, is due any day. Pauline and Ali will make the trip back to Mosul as soon as they know the baby is on the way. "And I hope next time you come, you can visit us in Mosul, and that everything will be back to normal, and we'll be home again," she says as she hugs me close in a warm and tight goodbye.

Four days later, on August 31, Pauline e-mails me to say:

Just a short note to let you know that Noor had her baby this morning at 10 a.m. She was in labour for six hours and she and the baby are doing well. He has a lot of black hair, is not bald as we'd expected he would be. He looks like Noor, weighs 3½ kgs, and has fair skin just like his mum.

14

Reunited in London

On a chilly, cloudy late summer Monday, the last bank holiday of the season, Margaret rose to an early alarm and listened, as usual, to the breakfast news broadcast on the radio. Prime Minister Tony Blair was back from his summer holiday in Barbados, and the talk was all about his renewed commitment to remaining at the country's helm despite a growing clamour for his resignation. Mr Blair's legacy was now inseparably linked to the Iraq debacle, and hearing the daily death roll reminded Margaret of the misery and stupidity of the whole venture, and, really, just made her feel tired. Today, the radio says, around sixty people have been killed in attacks across the country, including a suicide car bomb in Mosul. The total number of locals killed in the past four months, as followers of the Sunni and Shia sects wage war on each other and an apparently robust insurgency continues undiminished, is put at 10,000. Iraqi Prime Minister Nouri al-Maliki is insisting that the country "will never face civil war," and the British defence secretary, Des Brown, says things are getting better. So it must be OK.

Right now, though, she has other things on her mind, and Mr Blair's bleating reassurances that he intends to stay on in the premiership fade into the background as she pads about the multilevel apartment, trying to make some progress before the still-sleeping members of the family stir, and her youngest son returns home from his night-shift job. For days she has been getting ready to move her family across their South London street, from the flat that has become too cramped as their numbers have grown, to a large house, with four bedrooms and a garden, almost opposite. Amazing, she thinks as she places things in boxes, how much stuff they've managed to accumulate in the short time since they arrived in London. More amazing still is how, inside a year, Margaret has drawn her family together again, bringing them back under the same roof, alive and safe. Ten days shy of the first anniversary of the departure from her lovely home in Mosul, Margaret and her husband, their three boys and their maternal grandmother, Olive, are about to move into a real life. Weary as she is, Margaret is also delighted and excited. Everything she has wished and prayed for, over the past three and a half years, has finally come true.

Things hadn't looked so rosy in the weeks and months after Margaret landed back in the United Kingdom, feeling like a war refugee but, officially and realistically, simply a citizen returning home after a long stint abroad. Indeed, Margaret often despaired of ever making any headway as she tried to traverse the British bureaucracy, dealing with bored, and often taciturn, civil servants who told her she'd have been better off if she were an illegal immigrant, or an asylum seeker, someone utterly helpless and needy. Finding out what rights she had, and what assistance her two boys, Ali and Taleb, were entitled to, was an exhausting process. She was caught in the middle of the chicken-and-egg argument: without one official document to prove she existed, she couldn't get another, which she couldn't get unless she had the first. She needed somewhere to live, but had to have a credit history to satisfy the concerns of any prospective landlords that she could meet the rent. But without a fixed abode, she couldn't open a bank account, because the bank needed to see a utility bill showing that she was solvent at her current address. Foreigners in Saddam's Iraq were not permitted to hold overseas bank accounts, and in the mid-eighties had been forced to go through the motions of appearing to give up even the citizenship of their birth. Now they were here in London, British subjects in their homeland, Margaret, Ali and Taleb were expected to know how things worked and just get on with it. But Margaret had never had to do any of this before, and with nowhere to live, no job, no income and no bank account, with two sons and her incapacitated mother depending on her, one son still living in the Mosul war zone and her husband thousands of miles away in Yemen, sometimes she felt she must have swapped her own life for someone else's. "My sons and I felt really lonely here," she said, understating the impact of their forced upheaval. "After living in a close-knit society, it was difficult here, having left all our friends and family in Mosul."

She wore her chagrin, not as a cloak of self-pity, but as her duty. Now and then, she would tell me that she was "cheesed off" or had come down with what she called a "dose of the blues." It was more than natural. London is not a welcoming place; prices are high, jobs are difficult to find and employers can be mean. People rarely offer help, not really wanting to get involved in the lives of others, and are just as reticent, the boys found, about passing on information that could be useful. With an influx of young Europeans willing to work to improve their English, standards are low, and so are wages. Margaret was lost, but she felt obliged to maintain her equilibrium, sometimes through pursed lips and clenched teeth, to make sure the boys remained optimistic about their prospects in one of the world's truly great cities.

Both boys, but most especially Ali, found the changed circumstances much more difficult to deal with than Margaret had expected them to. She hadn't realized that, both being in their early twenties, they were old enough to be considered adults, but they were not yet mature enough to roll with the punches that might be delivered in life's new fight. The blow of having to leave their home had been compounded by profound culture shock. The concept of adulthood and independence is different in Arab society: sons remain at home with their parents, often for life, bringing their wives into the household to join the mother in a clutch of carers. In British society specifically and Western society generally, by contrast, young men of Ali and Taleb's age are expected to be pursuing independent lives. These young men had witnessed the destruction of the privilege they had believed to be their birthright, in a war of no meaning. And now they had not only to settle into a new and alien life, but also find what work they could in order to contribute to the collective family pot to make ends meet. In Mosul, Margaret said of her sons, "they were so used to being someone, and now they're no one, and it's difficult to settle."

Upon their arrival in London, Margaret, Olive and the boys stayed at the home of her brother, David, a primary school teacher. They squeezed into his divorcee's flat while they gauged the lay of the land. Ali had arrived a couple of months earlier and so had an idea of where things were and how they worked. He had found a job in a local store, initially stacking shelves, though his natural leadership qualities soon saw him promoted to assistant manager, and the extra responsibility and status suited him well. He investigated part-time computer engineering courses that would enable him to top up the degree he had brought with him from Mosul University, but which, because of the long-term international sanctions on Iraq, still left him well behind the developments of the industry worldwide.

He bombastically shared his half-formed opinions on everything from oil prices to Jesus, in a manner that simultaneously betrayed the failings of his education and his high self-regard. His mother had laughed when she'd told me that he had a healthy opinion of himself, pointing to the multiple photographs that Ali used as his laptop screen-saver. "I told you he likes himself," Margaret said when I asked Ali whether the photos were of his twin brother, Omar, still in Mosul, and was told: "No, it's me." As the eldest son, Ali took his machismo very seriously, acting as gatekeeper and host, but rarely helping his mother with such mundane tasks as grocery shopping and food preparation. Indeed, both he and Taleb seemed to snort through their delicate Arabian nostrils at the situation they now found themselves in, disapproving of such modern British phenomena as public binge-drinking and ubiquitously fashionable bare female midriffs, while selfishly wreathing the tiny flat in clouds of acrid cigarette smoke despite Margaret's constant, patient protestations that it made her feel ill.

Taleb appeared more easy-going than Ali, somewhat modest and certainly not as self-possessed. He tried a few jobs, mostly menial, such as helping out in a Turkish takeaway where he was shamefully underpaid, and wearing a shiny black suit to stand guard at the door of a Trafalgar Square nightclub. Eventually he settled for an overnight job at a furniture supplier, restocking the shelves; it paid well enough, he liked the other guys, and once he was made a permanent member of staff it gave him a platform from which to move on. It also, much to his mother's relief, gave him an appreciation of the value of education, and he began to think about returning to school, though to study what he hadn't yet decided. Improving his English seemed like a smart first step.

Margaret had brought with her about US$20,000, proceeds from the sale of land in a Yezidi village called Basheikar, not far from Mosul, that Zuhair had been granted by the government. The sale had gone through the day before they left, she said, "so I thought that was a sign from God and it meant everything was going to be OK." She'd had a soft spot for the land, she said, because the village was a melting pot of Iraq's religions, with mosques, churches and Yezidi temples, and appealed to her superstitious side. "The first year I was in Iraq, I went to see the place. There was a tree, and people who didn't have children tied a ribbon around the tree so that a child would come. There was no road then, you either had to walk or ride a donkey; I walked. I put a ribbon around the tree and I had Alia."

The money, transferred from Iraq to Jordan, where she collected it in cash, would see them through until they were earning their own keep. A large chunk went on paying the rent, six months in advance, on a flat that, while clean and bright, had steps up and down into every room, which made getting Olive to and from the bathroom a particularly complicated negotiation. Margaret fretted over the white carpets, but was pleased with the freshly renovated bathroom and kitchen. The flat was close to the railway station and a twenty-minute train journey from central London. Shops were just a stroll away and public transport was right outside the front door. David was close, too, and often dropped in on his way home.

"When I first came to England I did not expect it would be as difficult as it was to get into the system," Margaret said as she looked back on the year. "First of all the accommodation was hard to get and expensive. And it wasn't easy to find work as if you have not had experience of working in the UK then nobody is interested." The job she did find, at a private nursing home for elderly men and women, was tough going, with quite a bit of heavy lifting, which at one stage led to a back injury that landed her flat on her back for weeks. She also did a couple of night shifts a week, which inexplicably paid less than the day shift. Nevertheless, it was a short walk from home and she was in no position to turn it down.

∗

Zuhair came for Christmas 2005, taking time off from his teaching duties in Ibb. Alia came, too, from Amman, with her husband and toddler. The joy of the reunion was marred by news that a cousin had been caught "in the wrong place at the wrong time," in a firefight between American troops and armed gangs, and had been shot to death. "We were all terribly upset," Margaret wrote to me. "I remember the night before we left Iraq in the summer he came to say goodbye to Zuhair. He did not realize that I was travelling also, and was so upset he just kept saying 'what can I say?' He and his family were always very protective towards me. Then two weeks after that, another relative also died the same way."

These tragedies intensified her fears for Omar, still in Mosul finishing his studies. "I wish my son was out of Iraq as the situation gets worse day by day," she said. Omar took precautions, she said, as he was well aware of his potential as a target for kidnapping gangs, or thugs bent on anti-Ba'athist retribution. He checked the coast was clear each morning before he left for college, and on a couple of occasions had decided to stay at home after noticing an unfamiliar car parked outside the house with men in it whom he had never seen. He was in constant touch with his mother and father, by e-mail and Internet phone. Before Omar graduated with his degree in veterinary science, Margaret started popping into the veterinary surgeries that appeared to be as numerous as Indian restaurants in London – where people seem to like their pets more than they do other people – to find out about internships for him. Apart from having to decide which branch he would like to pursue, and choose between small animals – cats, dogs, hamsters – and large – horses, cows – it seemed that Omar had embarked upon the right professional path for success in Britain.

He graduated in late July and within days he had packed up his belongings and driven, with a couple of uncles, to the main Kurdish city of Irbil, from where he flew to Jordan and stayed for a day or so with his sister, Alia, in Amman. Then, on August 13, together with Alia's son, the siblings flew to London for an ecstatic reunion at Heathrow airport with their mother and brothers.

A week later, Zuhair arrived. He and Margaret had jumped through the Foreign Office hoops, both in London and in Sana'a, and he had been granted residency in the United Kingdom. He was head of his household once more. The al-Sharooks were together again as a family.

As she prepared the move into the new family house – for which she had to pay one year's rent in advance – Margaret's happiness was such that she found it difficult to revisit the difficulties of the past few years. She acknowledged that being apart from Zuhair for so long had been draining. And having to start her life again, when she and Zuhair should have been preparing for a comfortable retirement and contemplating a contented old age, surrounded by children and grandchildren, financial worries well behind them, was something she never could have imagined.

"At times I feel bitter as, at my age now, my husband and I should be quite settled and secure in our life, not having to worry and restart our life all over again," she told me. "On the other hand, I thank God that my family has the opportunity to be able to build their future in the UK as there is no future in Iraq. But my heart bleeds for the ones left behind.

"I do not regret anything," she concludes. "Life is what you make it. You have good and bad experiences and you learn from both. I think regret is a wasted emotion."

Epilogue

The woman identified in this book as Pauline asked me not to use her real name because Iraq is no longer a safe place to live. As a foreigner, she feels more vulnerable than most. So her name here is a pseudonym, as are the names I have used for her husband and children, and all their relatives and friends. Their lives are tainted by fear that crept in when the coalition forces that invaded Iraq in 2003 opened the door to an era themed "freedom."

It is clear now, even to the President of the United States and the British prime minister, who are responsible for the war in Iraq, that the consequences of their actions – and lies – have been utterly devastating for that country. My aim in writing this book was not to rake over the coals of the political manipulations and machinations that led to the March 2003 invasion of Iraq and the removal of the regime of Saddam Hussein. Rather, I wished to investigate the life lived by ordinary Iraqi people through the eyes of two women whose perspectives straddle the cultural, racial, linguistic, religious and geographic lines dividing Iraq itself. Often these barriers present insurmountable obstacles to understanding of the country's complexities. By allowing us into their lives, Pauline and Margaret have become interpreters of an existence glimpsed only through headlines and horror stories, which often so belie comprehension that many people just give up; they turn the page, change the channel and resort to glib judgements.

What is happening in Iraq today can be traced in a straight line to the declaration of war on the world by fanatical Islamic ideologues on September 11, 2001 – and, beyond, to Saddam Hussein's invasion of Kuwait, the first Gulf War of 1991, and the subsequent personalization of his interaction with the then president of the United States, George H. W. Bush. Within hours of the attacks on New York and Washington in 2001, senior officers of the American government, many of whom had served the elder Bush and believed in the supremacy of a US empire, made it clear that once they had dealt with the perpetrators of those terrorist acts they intended to topple Saddam. The Iraqi dictator had nothing to do with religious radicalism. He had no links to Al Qaeda. He had sought to build Iraq into a modern and secular, strongly nationalistic state. He apparently didn't even have any weapons of mass destruction left over from his earlier arsenal. He had bluff, which was about to be called. And thus his country, with its vast oil reserves, was up for grabs.

The ideological justification, in Washington and London, for the 2003 war was a supposition – later shown to be based on information that its promoters knew to be false – that Iraq posed a threat to the Western world. The theory went that by remaking the rogue state, its threat would be removed. It also supposed that in doing so, a strong message of deterrence would be sent to other potential staging posts of terrorism and that a troublesome region of the world would be brought to heel. That the war would also allow the United States to lay down some oil credits to help bankroll the ghost-busting venture known as the "war on terror" was an added bonus.

Blinded as they were by their own self-righteousness, and preoccupied with the task of selling their venture to increasingly sceptical constituents, the coalition leaders were intellectually ill prepared for the outcome of their own actions. They possessed little understanding of the reality of tyranny, and seemed to genuinely believe that Iraqi people could just discard the straitjacket of dictatorship that had bound them so long, and slip immediately into a modern democratic, peaceful and tolerant state.

Decision-making and initiative on this scale, however, rarely feature in the landscape of autocracy. Few people in Iraq had real knowledge or understanding of themselves beyond their status as subjects of the socialist state machine. To interpret themselves in any other way had been a crime in a country run by a man whose policies aimed to remould the national identity to the exclusion of individuality. But now, if a man is no longer a subject of the Ba'ath Party, a loyal supporter of Saddam Hussein or a hostile dissident, what is he? How does he define himself – by his religion? His sect? His tribe? His ethnicity? By his village or his region? In relation to his neighbour, or to his enemy? Until March, 2003, Iraqis were encouraged to define themselves by the enemies without. Now they have turned inward, and on each other, in their quest to expunge the hate, and the shame, that was nurtured as a mark of their belonging to the Iraqi nation. We are now seeing, in Iraq, a concentration of the struggle to answer one of the key questions of our time, as competing interpretations of what is right are fighting for supremacy at the expense of the universal good. It is what former US President Bill Clinton has called the "values crisis," in which common humanity vies with absolute truth.

Iraq's civil war will find its own end. Among the vast array of the invaders' arrogant follies, perhaps the one that has been most damaging in its impact was the assumption that their own national interests and notions of what is right and just, from which Iraqi people had long been isolated by Saddam's government, were paramount. As subsequent events have illustrated, these concerns were not shared by Iraqis. Now that they are working out their own interests, albeit in a horrific bloodletting, we are compelled to await the final outcome wrought within each of Iraq's many, and disparate, communities. It is impossible to predict how long this process will take. Nor is it likely that it can be influenced, let alone foreshortened, from outside. It must reach its own conclusion, through predestined violence and death.

The only reason this book is not marred by a final tragedy is because both of the Englishwomen whose stories it tells were able to leave the inevitable theatre of civil collapse. Pauline, because she married a Kurd, escaped to the relative normality of northern Iraq's self-protective Kurdish region. Margaret sponsored her husband's emigration to the United Kingdom so their family could be reunited. From the safety of their new lives, both women worry daily about those whom they have left behind in Mosul. For them, the struggle is over; now they are condemned to watch it from afar.

Margaret and Pauline have my deepest gratitude for their patience and cooperation, as well as my enduring respect for what they have been able to achieve in circumstances beyond the comprehension of most of their compatriots. Pauline and Ali were gracious and generous hosts when I visited them in Iraq in mid-2006; I offer my apologies for any stress I caused them with my presence, and heartfelt thanks for their warm welcome and hospitality. Jamal put his formidable technical expertise to good use in sourcing photographs and information about old Mosul, for which I am indebted. I enjoyed occasional visits to Margaret's home in South London, when she made me tea, of course, and regaled me with stories of her life in Iraq. I wish the whole family the very best of luck in making a new life in what can be a cold, indifferent and difficult city. I've no doubt all the family will find the success and happiness they deserve.

My friend and boss at AFP in Hong Kong, Phil Chetwynd, and Eric Wishart, the agency's regional director, made the project possible by setting precedents that gave me time and space to get on with it. Peter Murtagh, now managing editor at the *Irish Times*, assigned me to cover the war in Iraq. Bruce Grill and Marie-Noelle Viallis-Grill always seemed to sweep in at just the right moment with fine food and wine, and conversation and encouragement. Other thanks go to James Denselow at Chatham House/King's College in London for some help with fact checking. Damien McElroy was patient, supportive, helpful and loving, as always. Martin Liu at Cyan was unflagging in his enthusiasm for and belief in the value of the idea. As were my parents, Edward and Bette O'Donnell. To all, thank you.

Names of people and places appear as they do in most news reports. Any mistakes are my own.

Bibliography

Books

Aburish, Taleb K., *Saddam Hussein, the Politics of Revenge* (Bloomsbury, London, 2000).

Ala Bashir, *The Insider: Trapped in Saddam's Brutal Regime* (Abacus, London, 2005).

Anderson, Jon Lee, *The Fall of Baghdad* (Abacus, London, 2006).

BBC News, *The Battle for Iraq: BBC News Correspondents on the War against Saddam and a New World Agenda* (BBC, London, 2003).

Bodanksy, Yossef, *The Secret History of the Iraq War* (Regan Books, New York, 2004).

Champdor, Albert, *Babylon* (Elek Books, London, 1958).

Clawson, Patrick (ed.), *How to Build a New Iraq after Saddam* (Washington Institute of Near East Policy, Washington, 2002).

Dabrowska, Karen, *Iraq: The Bradt Travel Guide* (Bradt Travel Guides, London, 2002).

Farouk-Sluglett, Marion and Peter Sluglett, *Iraq since 1958: From Revolution to Dictatorship* (I. B. Taurus, London/New York, 2001).

Goldfarb, Michael, *Ahmad's War, Ahmad's Peace, Surviving under Saddam, Dying in the New Iraq* (Carroll & Graf, New York, 2005).

Hartung, William D., *How Much Are You Making on the War, Daddy? A Quick and Dirty Guide to War Profiteering in the Bush Administration* (Nation Books, New York, 2003).

Hersh, Seymour M., *Chain of Command* (Penguin, New York, 2005).

Hiro, Dilip, *Iraq: A Report from the Inside* (Granta Books, London, 2003).

Hiro, Dilip, *Secrets and Lies: The True Story of the Iraq War* (Politico's, London, 2005).

Johnson, Chalmers, *Blowback: The Costs and Consequences of American Empire* (Time Warner, London, 2002).

Karsh, Efraim and Inari Rautsi, *Saddam Hussein: A Political Biography* (Grove Press, New York, 1991).

Klare, Michael, *Blood and Oil: How America's Thirst for Petrol Is Killing Us* (Penguin, London, 2005).

Mansfield, Peter, *A History of the Middle East* (Penguin, London, 2003).

Newby, Gordon D., *A Concise Encyclopedia of Islam* (One World Publications, Oxford, 2002).

Nuha al-Radi, *Baghdad Diaries 1991–2002* (Saqi Books, London, 2003).

Packer, George, *The Assassins' Gate: America in Iraq* (Faber & Faber, London, 2006).

Parenti, Christian, *The Freedom: Shadows and Hallucinations in Occupied Iraq* (New Press, New York/London, 2004).

Polk, William R., *Understanding Iraq: The Whole Sweep of Iraqi History from Genghis Khan's Mongols to the Ottoman Turks to the British Mandate to the American Occupation* (Harper Perennial, New York/London, 2006).

Porter, Jadranka, *Under Siege in Kuwait: A Survivor's Story* (Gollancz, London, 1991).

Reeva Spector, Simon and Eleanor H. Tejirian (eds), *The Creation of Iraq, 1914–1921* (Columbia University Press, New York, 2004).

Rhea Nemet-Nejat, Karen, *Daily Life in Ancient Mesopotamia* (Hendrickson Publishers, MA, 2002).

Ricks, Thomas E., *Fiasco: The American Military Adventure in Iraq* (Allen Lane, London, 2006).

Rogers, Paul, *Iraq and the War on Terror, Twelve Months of Insurgency, 2004/2005* (I. B. Tauris, London/New York, 2006).

Salam Pax, *The Baghdad Blog* (Atlantic Books, London, 2003).

Seierstad, Asne, *A Hundred and One Days: A Baghdad Journal* (Virago, London, 2004).

Shields, Sarah D., *Mosul before Iraq: Like Bees Making Five-sided Cells* (State University of New York Press, 2000).

Stark, Freya, *Baghdad Sketches* (Marlboro Press, Northwestern, IL, 2000).
White, Andrew, *Iraq: Searching for Hope* (Continuum, London/New York, 2005).
Wright, Evan, *Generation Kill* (Corgi, London, 2005).
Zizek, Slavoj, *Iraq: The Borrowed Kettle* (Verso, London/New York, 2005).

Also
Various work on the history of the Lancashire textile industry by Emeritus Professor Stanley Chapman, University of Nottingham.

Journals/newspapers

Agenzia Fides
"Life is a nightmare for Christians in Mosul," October 14, 2004.

AlertNet
"Facing threats, local doctors flee Mosul," May 1, 2006.

Associated Press
"In Mosul, a new Iraqi council tries to heal rifts, purge Saddam loyalists," by Louis Meixler, May 15, 2003.

The Atlantic
"Blind into Baghdad," by James Fallows, January/February, 2004.
"Spies, lies and weapons: what went wrong," by Kenneth M. Pollack, January/February, 2004.
"The tragedy of Tony Blair," by Geoffrey Wheatcroft, June, 2004.
"Jihad 2.0," by Nadya Labi, July/August, 2006.
"Inventing Al-Zarqawi," by Mary Anne Weaver, July/August, 2006.

bbc.co.uk
"Iraq hostages: facts & figures," March 4, 2005.

DailyIndia.com
"Killing, kidnap force Iraq brain drain," April 17, 2006 (citing UPI).

Daily Telegraph
"US troops stretched to limit as insurgents fight back," by Robin Gedye, November 13, 2004.
"Killings lead to brain drain from Iraq," by Oliver Poole, May 14, 2006.

Independent
"Once they called it a model for the occupation: has the US lost control of Mosul?" by Patrick Cockburn, December 17, 2004.

Institute of War and Peace Reporting (Iraq Crisis Report no. 2)
"Analysis: End of the party: regime change is not enough – a sustained programme of de-Ba'athification is essential to rid Iraq of the influence of the ruling party and its functionaries," by Ali A. Allawi, March 6, 2003.

International Herald Tribune
"Swept up in a storm," by Paul Krugman, February 25/26, 2006.
"Sectarian divide intensifies in Iraq," by Jeffrey Gettleman, March 27, 2006.
"In Iraq, a zone of hedonism and safety," by Robert F. Worth, April 22/23, 2006.
"Three Iraqs would be one big problem," by Anthony H. Cordesman, May 10, 2006.
"Lost after translation," by Basim Mardan, November 21, 2006.
"Republic of dreams," by Omar Chanim Fathi, November 21, 2006.
"Fear of freedom," by Waddah Ali, November 21, 2006.

IRINnews.org
"Iraq: NGOs' report puts kidnappings this year at 20,000," April 20, 2006.

Kurdistan Observer
"In Mosul, a new Iraqi council tries to heal rifts, purge Saddam loyalists," May 15, 2003 (citing AP).

New York Times
"'Liberty or death' is a grim option for the local councils in Iraq's young democracy," by Dexter Filkins, February 15, 2004.
"Kidnapped in Iraq: victim's tale of clockwork death and ransom," by Kirk Semple, May 4, 2006.

New Yorker
"Who lied to whom: did the administration endorse a forgery about Iraq's nuclear program?" by Seymour M. Hersh, March 31, 2003.

Newsweek
"Our man in Mosul," by Joshua Hammer, January 28, 2004.
"Wrap these guys up," by Christian Caryl & John Barry, December 8, 2005.

Reuters
"University president wants only peshmergas to save shattered Mosul University," by Daren Butler, April 24, 2003.
"Mosul: from order to mayhem," November 18, 2004.

Strykernews.com
"Gunmen kidnap the Catholic archbishop of Mosul as pre-election violence flares in Iraq," January 18, 2005 (citing *New York Times*).

The Telegraph (Calcutta)
"History repeats itself in Mosul," April 26, 2003 (citing Reuters).

Wall Street Journal
"How Iraqi professor overcame doubts to trust a general," by Hugh
    Pope, November 3, 2003.

Websites

AReporter.com (for the table in Chapter 8 which appeared on this
    Boston-based website in April, 2003. With thanks to Constantine
    von Hoffman)
Durham.gov.uk
Encyclopedia Brittanica online
Globalpolicy.org
GlobalSecurity.com
Newcastle.icnetwork.co.uk
Pendletourism.com
Wikipedia.com